I want to tell you that I found your book totally BRIL ̱ingly insightful and resonated with me so powerfully. You have got it so right! I wish your book had been around when I was at the Guildhall - I would have found it a huge help. I hope it will become required reading for all music students everywhere in future. That kind of self-knowledge is invaluable...

Ann Mackay, soprano

Music From The Inside Out is an excellent book! It's an invaluable source of practical advice for anyone who is engaged in the endlessly fascinating process of playing a musical instrument. There will be something illuminating in the book for all musicians, regardless of their experience or level of ability.

William Howard, Schubert Ensemble

It's a hugely helpful and informative guide to performance. I loved it and will return to it again and again.

James Rhodes, pianist

Charlotte offers insights into the psychology of performing and practising that are completely invaluable. There is so much in this book that will resonate with any musician or instrumental teacher - it's wonderful!

David Angel, Maggini Quartet

MUSIC FROM THE INSIDE OUT

a musician's guide to freeing performance

Charlotte Tomlinson

To all my students who have been a constant inspiration over the years, without whom this book could not have been written

Acknowledgements

I would like to thank the following people:

Judy Dendy for her superb content editing and tireless commitment to high standards. She consistently managed to bring coherence and structure to all my ideas with unfailing support and good humour.

Jay and Terry Brightwater whose wisdom and emotional intelligence over the years have inspired me in the approach that I have taken in writing the book.

Daniel Davis, Miranda Flint, Jonathon Swinard, Kim Reilly, Samantha Ward, Lucy Dendy, Tom Butcher and Lucy Hare for reading my manuscript and for providing valuable insights.

Alexander Massey who was the first person to help me clarify what I wanted to write through recording interviews and making videos of my work.

Rachel Ingram for her meticulous proofreading.

My parents who have constantly supported me and have always believed I could write, even when I thought I couldn't.

Preface

I've written this book for all musicians, whether students, amateurs or professionals in the classical music world. I've developed generic principles that a wide range of classical musicians will relate to, whether instrumentalists or singers. I'm focusing on the person as a performer, rather than the type of musician they are or the type of instrument they play. This doesn't in any way exclude all the other genres of music – I would hope that rock and pop musicians, jazz musicians and any others would find something of value for themselves.

My intention is that the reader should read from the beginning to the end as key ideas have been developed through the chapters. The final chapter, for example, will be a lot more meaningful if the reader has absorbed what has gone before. But it is equally valid to dip in and out because most of the chapters will successfully stand on their own.

My experience has been drawn from my many years of teaching and performing the piano. I have now pulled all this together and work with musicians in a new and different capacity. Just as the horse whisperer listens to and draws out the essence of a horse, I've developed an equivalent skill in drawing out the essence of a musician, enabling them to play to their full potential. Hence "Music from the Inside Out". All the case studies are based on true stories and are from my own experience. Because of this they are largely, but not exclusively, focused on pianists. I have changed names in each instance.

Table of Contents

Introduction

*A*re you performing to the peak of your ability? Are you expressing yourself fully from your heart and soul? Are you playing "music from the inside out"?

This book is written for any classical musician who has suffered from performance nerves, who struggles with tensions, aches and pains, or who battles with issues of confidence and self-belief.

If you know that pain, anxiety and confusion, then read on. There is hope; it doesn't need to be like this.

Sergei, a 21-year old virtuoso pianist, came to me some time ago with pains in his wrists that had rendered him virtually unable to play. He and his family had left their home in Eastern Europe for the UK when he was sixteen, with the aim of having the best piano tuition he could, to prepare to go to music college and pursue his dreams of becoming a soloist. But despite his best efforts, he failed to get a place at any of the colleges; the pains he was having put a stop to him practising for anything more than thirty minutes a day. When I saw him, he was desperate. He had spent five years trying to get himself better so he could play again. He had seen GPs, osteopaths, acupuncturists and physiotherapists; he had practised and not practised; he had had cortisone injections and had been advised to have an operation, but nothing was working. He had no awareness at all of why he was suffering in the way he was, and thought it was simply a physical problem.

What he needed was someone to join the dots, to help him see that there was an array of complex emotional and psychological issues behind the physical symptoms.

He needed someone to help him unravel these issues, understand them and then support him in taking the steps towards building healthier physical habits and healthier ways of thinking. This is the way I worked with Sergei. This is the way I have worked with an enormous number of musicians over the years. And I've seen it work, time and time again.

I believe profoundly that if the musical passion is not flowing through a talented musician, we need to understand and work with the 'whole person'.

I had the beginnings of tendonitis as a piano student at music college and it was enough to shock me into action. I felt compelled to get to the bottom of it. Why was it happening? I thought I was enjoying myself. I really loved playing music, I was keen to work and do well, and I loved the stimulation of working with other fabulous singers and players. What I hated was the endless pressure and what felt like constant judgement from all around. I wasn't happy, but I was barely aware of it. On some level I felt that I would be shown up as a failure, as someone who didn't have what it takes to be a professional performer. I needed to understand that there was a connection between my feelings and the inflamed tendons in my arms.

As a professional player and teacher, I started exploring. I wanted to find out more. I studied Alexander Technique, Tai Chi, Yoga and Feldenkrais; I took courses in different types of bodywork so that I could understand the body better and how it reacted to stress. I delved into the whole arena of personal development, fascinated by the connections between our mind, emotions and body. I had the bit between my teeth and I wouldn't let it go. Increasingly my discoveries started influencing my teaching. I spotted musicians with problems even before they knew themselves, helping to get to the root of them before they took hold. Musicians I was working with were starting to get better, were feeling happier, enjoying music more and were playing with delight and freedom. It was inspiring! I began to realise that within me was a real desire to make connections, to see the big picture, and that I love helping other people find that for themselves.

The symptoms are just what show on the surface; if the symptoms are treated in isolation, they will return. It is the big picture that counts.

Over the years I have known musicians who have battled with injury and many others who have struggled to overcome crippling performance anxiety. Some issues were just irritating niggles, some led to breakdowns. I have seen the pain, confusion and desperation just below the surface in so many musicians. It doesn't need to be like this.

In our culture, judgement underpins everything. Learning to play an instrument to professional standards is unbelievably demanding. You need skill, commitment and discipline; you need to master your instrument, faithfully interpret the music you are playing, manage your nerves and above all, be free enough to express yourself. And if you are doing this in a culture that has judgement at its core, there are consequences: judgement is dangerous.

Judgement feeds something that I call the Inner Critic, and this Inner Critic can be devastating.

It says to you, "You can't do it. You're no good. You're just a fraud." Or it says, "Oh my God, I just made a mistake!" and your hand tenses up.

When I was at music college, I was amazed to witness what students would accept from their teachers. Very often, it would be those same teachers who were considered the 'good' teachers, the ones the students would clamour to study with. Without a doubt, those teachers had fantastic knowledge to share, but I also heard students being told how 'bad' they were, how they would never amount to anything, picking out some personal characteristics and criticising them. It was not uncommon for students to leave their lessons in tears. I still hear those stories today.

It is distressing to see sensitive, talented musicians suffering, when what they need is understanding, support and help to overcome their fears, overcome their Inner Critic, and overcome any physical problems they may have. If this could be you, rest assured: you are not alone. There is nothing wrong with you; you are not broken and you don't need to be fixed. It is possible for you to learn how to free up both physically and emotionally in a way that will enhance your playing. You can also move into a realm where you have never gone before, so not only can you play to the peak of your ability, but you can play from your heart and soul – with musical fire!

In Chapter 1 we look at the root of playing "music from the inside out": Motivation.

1

Whose motivation is it anyway?

> *Without inspiration the best powers of the mind remain dormant.*
> *There is a fuel in us which needs to be ignited with sparks.*
> **Johann Gottfried Von Herder**

Li Ping was brought up in Shanghai, China, and started having piano lessons when she was three years old. She told me that her first teacher had regularly picked her up physically and hit her when she hadn't performed up to his exacting standards. She showed no distress when she told me about it. It was clearly something that she considered normal behaviour and she had seen it around her all the time. The physical beating was part of an overly strong structure that her teacher had used to keep her in line and make sure she was making progress according to his standards. When she started having lessons with me in England at the age of thirteen, she floundered. The strict structure she had been used to was no longer there.

I knew she had been surviving on a motivation that had come from avoiding criticism and impressing her teacher, and I wanted her to find her own.

For two years, she barely practised. She made excuses, she played with the idea of practising, but achieved very little. It was frustrating to see someone who wanted to be a professional musician do next to no practice for so long. It was extremely tempting to lay down the law to get her to do something. Instead I waited; but I continued to listen to her, talk to her and help build up her sense of self-worth. I believed in her. She had never been encouraged or told that she played well by any of her previous teachers, so I encouraged each and every tiny step of progress she made, trusting that she would eventually find her own love for music. It was a slow process. After two years she started to practise again, and then she practised with a verve and commitment I hadn't seen before. She was playing fantastically well, with a newfound passion for music, and was taking herself by surprise. She felt newly motivated, and this time her new passion was coming from inside her. Now it was her own.

Motivation starts from you

It is so important to be motivated.

It sounds so simple, but a stunning performance doesn't just result from a good technique, notes in the right place and a good interpretation of the music. It comes from the performer themselves, from their passion for the music and for their instrument.

This is what you need to carry you through the challenges of preparing for the music profession, and of course, the stresses and strains of being a professional musician. The demands are high, and without your own love and passion for what you are doing, you may find you can't sustain the level of commitment you need.

Your motivation can't be someone else's because at some point it will show.

Deep down you know whether you want to be playing music or you don't. You also know whether that desire is yours or whether it has come from someone else. The truth always comes out at some point.

- *Who motivated you as a child?*
- *Who or what motivates you now?*
- *Are you like Li Ping, dependent on a strong structure or a single personality for your motivation?*

When Li Ping was discovering on an unconscious level where her own personal motivation lay, she dragged her heels and didn't practise. Practice needs to be something you get up in the morning to do because it inspires you and enriches you. The desire to practise comes from your desire to play music and to express yourself. I am always inspired when I chat to a friend of mine, a wise, experienced pianist in his nineties. He told me of his passion for Scarlatti sonatas and how it was the thought of practising them that got him out of bed in the morning. It is no surprise that he has reached his nineties, because his motivation for music and living is so strong!

Practising needs to be your desire and no one else's. If I see someone not wanting to practise, the warning bells start ringing. I see this as that person questioning their relationship with their instrument and music. Equally, if they start changing lessons just a few too many times or missing them entirely, oversleeping, missing buses or any other reasons for not showing up to their commitment, it will be something to do with their motivation. The best thing to do is to bring it up to conscious awareness

7

before circumstances force you there: who or what motivates you, and is it what you really want to do?

The pressure cooker

Guy was sixteen and came to piano lessons reluctantly and with his head down. We laughed a lot in lessons, and he clearly enjoyed playing the piano and the lesson itself. What he didn't like was feeling he had to play the piano. He felt the pressure of his music scholarship and all that it entailed, and it started weighing down on him. When I gave him permission to have a full three weeks off in the summer with no piano whatsoever, he was over the moon. He had always practised for long hours and had never been allowed to have a summer break before. This break proved to be more than a break. It gave him time to consider what he really felt about the piano, and to his parents' horror, he decided to give it up completely and the music scholarship along with it.

When he rang me to explain, he told me he had had enough. He had felt pushed from one exam and competition to another for his entire life, with no time and space for 'him' in the mix. He had been pushed to his limits, and his own internal elastic band had snapped along with his own inner motivation to play the piano. It was so intense that he felt he had to give up. He didn't want to play the piano because playing the piano was what he was doing to please his parents and not himself. Ironically, the time when he really found his inner motivation was when he said to his parents: "No! Enough is enough!"

It took Guy some years to start playing the piano again. I was delighted that he did come back to it, as well as being a little surprised. The strength of emotion he felt when he stopped could easily have taken him decades to move on from. The second time round was a completely different situation. He was tentative and a little nervous, but over time, both through starting lessons again and finding a duet partnership, he developed a love for the piano that nourished him in a way that it never did the first time round.

There is great value in asking yourself questions in order to bring to the surface important issues that you may not have been aware of.

- *Do you feel as if you have been in the pressure cooker, pushed and pressurised without having your say?*
- *What could you do to regain your own motivation? How could you now give yourself different options and choices that serve you better?*

Staking your claim

Your motivation needs to be yours. Your passion and desire to play needs to be yours too. It doesn't work if that desire is second hand, something you think you should feel because your parents, your teacher or anyone else thinks you should feel it. It is not up to them. Sometimes it can take time for you to clarify your own motivation for playing when it is closely linked with someone else's desire for you. When a teacher, a parent or someone close to you wants a lot for you, however well meaning that might be, it can be confusing. You want to play but they want you to play too. It is as if they are instilling motivation into you. And where are you in all that? This is exactly what happened to Anna.

Anna's rebellion

Anna was a seventeen-year-old student who was well on the way to a successful performing career as a cellist. She loved performing, she loved the cello, but she was confused. She was an only child and the apple of her parents' eye. They came to every concert, driving her round the country if necessary to give her all the opportunities they felt she needed to perform. She started reacting and playing up. She stopped practising, she gave concerts that were well below her ability and her studies started suffering.

Anna was finding her parents' interest and support suffocating, and without being fully aware of what she was doing, she was sabotaging her own progress by trying to get them off her back.

Her own motivation to play the cello was starting to get muddled with her parents' motivation for her, and her reactions were one way of trying to find her own motivation again. Anna eventually made a break from her parents by studying abroad, where, by having lessons with a new, inspirational teacher and being part of a fantastic string quartet, she gradually found a way to rekindle her own love for the cello. She stopped reacting and started her own life, practising and playing for the love of it and because she wanted to.

Think about what motivates you as a musician.

- *How can you separate your own motivation from other people around you?*
- *How can you make your motivation your own?*

Separating yourself and your own interests, desires and passions from those of people close to you is critical. When you are deeply committed to the process of learning a musical instrument to professional standards, there is often a heavy involvement from parents and teachers in the early stages. That support is critical. Without it, it is a much harder challenge to reach the standards you are hoping for. But sometimes things can get a little muddled and problems arise. This is when the teacher or parent, usually unconsciously, puts their own needs and issues first, sometimes even living their own unlived life through the person in question.

Carrying someone else's unfulfilled desires

Liz was a student who had a particularly complicated relationship with her mother. She was a talented eighteen-year-old pianist who had just been given scholarships to three of the London music colleges. Soon after the news of the scholarships, she started suffering from tendonitis in her arms. Playing was becoming more and more painful. She was extremely distressed by this and we began a long process in our lessons of undoing the physical tensions and exploring what was triggering the tendonitis. Things started to improve in fits and starts, but Liz was not happy.

She had no belief in herself or her ability, despite the scholarships and enormous reassurance from all around that she was a very fine pianist with a promising future.

During one particularly memorable conversation, she told me that she didn't believe she could go anywhere with the piano because she simply was not good enough. When I pressed her further on this, she told me she wasn't really sure that she wanted to be a professional pianist at all. This shocked her because she had had no idea up to this point that she was even thinking in this way. And yet her emotional response was clearly showing that something was bubbling up under the surface.

Her mother was giving her mixed messages. On one hand, Liz's mother wanted her daughter to be successful and was obviously proud of what Liz had achieved. On the other hand, she would make subtly undermining comments saying how hard it was to get anywhere in the music profession and ask why Liz was even bothering. Liz told me that her mother had desperately wanted to go to music college herself, but instead had got married and had had children very young, stopping all her involvement with music. As Liz told me this, she started to smile, suddenly realising what had happened. She had felt her mother's distress at not having continued her musical studies and had unconsciously decided to live her musical life for her mother, by doing what her mother had always wanted to do.

Once she realised this, she knew she had to make her own choices independent of her mother and to live her own life. Just knowing that the choices were hers to make and hers alone, changed Liz's life significantly. She gave herself permission not to go to music college if she really didn't want to, something she had never even considered before. Her tendonitis started to clear up and Liz looked a lot happier. After a few weeks, she decided that she really did want to be a professional musician and that music college was the route she wanted to take. That decision had been hers, possibly for the very first time.

• If you, like Liz, have lost your motivation, could you risk letting everything go so that you can find where your real passion lies?

What real motivation looks like!

A group of street kids from Venezuela were once given a chance to learn a music instrument, and then an orchestra was founded to give those kids an opportunity to take their playing to another level. That orchestra, the Simon Bolivar Orchestra, performs with a degree of passion and vitality that is often lacking in professional orchestras. At their BBC Prom concert a few years ago, they were met by rapturous applause from musicians and non-musicians alike.

Clearly there is something very powerful about coming from a difficult background where life is tough. Being part of an orchestra must seem like heaven in comparison to fending for yourself on the streets. I heard of a music school in Kampala, the capital city of Uganda, which frequently had to deal with the problems of vandalism. Windows would be smashed on a regular basis. But these smashed windows were in reality not the result of vandalism at all. They were broken by children who were breaking in to the music school late at night to practise!

Many musicians came over to the West from the Soviet Union around the time of the collapse in Communism. The difficulties and lack of freedom that they had encountered in the Soviet Union provided them with a strong motivation to be somewhere they could express themselves freely.

The motivation in all these stories is strong and powerful. It is as if it lights a fire within you, inspiring you to your best. No one chooses to live in difficult circumstances or to have the type of restrictions the former Soviets had, but such hardships do create a spark of desire that that those of us born in the privileged West have to search harder for.

Flattery is fickle

A less healthy way of being motivated is by needing attention and flattery from other people as a result of your talent and your performances. This is as dangerous as relying on other people to be motivated for you, or allowing them to live their life through you. Flattery is fickle. The people who give it may change their mind at any moment and it can turn into something much more negative; or you may not get it when you expect it and want it.

It is disempowering to be dependent on flattery.
How much better not to need it at all!

Being motivated from needing attention also leads you into pleasing other people rather than pleasing yourself, or as in David's case, pleasing some ideal out there – that he should be playing Baroque music.

"But I should play Bach!"

David wasn't practising. He had tried with all the best intentions, but he couldn't get himself down to any real form of practice. He was puzzled, because he loved the piano, but when I pressed him further he told me that he didn't feel inspired to learn the Bach Prelude and Fugue he had said he wanted to learn. I asked him why he had decided that he wanted to learn it, and he said that he felt he should learn Bach.

He loved Romantic music but felt he was spending too much time immersed in learning the Romantics and that he should balance his repertoire with more Baroque and Classical.

I asked him to stop and think for a minute about what he loved about the piano, and when he had last relished going to the piano to practise. He shut his eyes to recollect, and then smiled. He told me it was when he had become riveted by the composer, Nicolai Medtner, a contemporary of Rachmaninov. He had loved Medtner's piano music and had spent hours listening to it and learning some of his more demanding pieces. There he was back again, reliving his enthusiasm. He left the lesson with a spring in his step and with the intention of once more immersing himself in Medtner, listening and learning. The piano had become his ally. He was looking forward to practising again.

David's argument was extremely reasonable. Of course when you are studying it is sensible to balance out the repertoire you are learning so that it covers a wide range; but not at the cost of your love for music and the instrument. Your inner self can only follow logic for so long, and then it will rebel. It might be quiet as in David's case, but it is still a form of rebellion.

In the name of duty

Let's take the young professional who does everything right. She practises, she does well in competitions, she gives good recitals. Everyone is pleased with her. She seems to have the ideal life. She fulfils her duty, and yet something is missing. Maybe for months, sometimes years there is an internal split which goes partially unrecognised and then she wakes up to the fact that she no longer enjoys playing. Why and how can this have happened? She loved it as a child and in her early years as a student, but now she can't face it. The pressures of being a musician, the politics of the music world and all the things that *aren't* playing music, have become too much. So she takes a break, a form of sabbatical from playing, risking losing her contacts in the musical world but desperately needing to regain the love that she once had. It is a common story.

It is no surprise that many musicians retrain and change career at a certain point because they have lost their joy in making music.

More often than not, the break works for them, and they find themselves drawn back into the world of music again, finding strategies for managing all the pressures in order to pursue what they know truly brings them alive.

Summary

If you recognise yourself in any of these stories, and realise that you've been carrying someone else's motivation, here are some steps you can take.

- **The first step** is awareness. Bring to the surface what or who it is that really motivates you to play or sing. Decide if that feels right or not.

- **The second step** is to remind yourself of what you love about your instrument and music, in the way David did. What inspires you about music? Why did you choose it?

- **The third step** is to relate those good feelings to any wavering realisations about motivation. Carrying someone else's motivation will not serve you. Do what you feel right to claim your own.

You will feel a tremendous sense of relief and freedom when what motivates you to play or sing is coming from within you.

In the next chapter we will look at one of the greatest enemies of motivation: the Bully.

2

The Bully

I remember an incident at music college when a friend of mine stood up to perform in front of her year group. She was nervous and felt under scrutiny. She was particularly nervous about performing in front of the person taking the class, who also happened to be her teacher. The teacher in question felt it was somehow their right as the teacher to say exactly what they felt about their student performing in a class situation.

My friend walked up onto the stage and before she even started to perform, her teacher said: "What do you think you look like? You look like a cripple!" My friend braced herself and carried on. She was used to it.

This is the Bully, the ogre who attacks from outside under the guise of educator and guide. The Bully can attack in a blatantly obvious way as in this story, or it can be more subtle, as the educator who has high standards – but at the cost of the student. The Bully need not even be a person, and can show itself through the pressure of commonly held belief systems such as perfectionism. People feel they have to buy into these belief systems because they are the norm and because everyone else is doing the same thing.

Physical and verbal bullying

The most obvious form of bullying comes in the form of physical and verbal attack. It is now less common to hear stories of students being hit because they have not performed up to standard, but it does still happen. Think of Li Ping, who was hit from the age of three when she made mistakes. Sergei, who I mentioned in the Introduction, was similarly hit across the hand on a regular basis when he hadn't performed to the level expected of him. He had also never, in twelve years of study, heard a teacher encourage him or tell him how good he was. It was hardly surprising that his body had seized up.

Verbal attacks are much more common. Teachers get frustrated because their students are not at the standard they expect and they lash out. "You are not working hard enough. You can't play and you are not going to make it," I heard one teacher say to a student, who promptly leaned against the wall in despair.

"And you have no confidence either," the teacher continued to say. In my language, this is abuse.

It is not generally seen as abuse, and it is still accepted in music colleges around the world. Students believe this is the 'right thing', and put up with it because the teacher has good ideas about music and technique, and has a good reputation, drawing in students internationally. That somehow allows the behaviour to continue despite the massive repercussions on the student.

Musicians need to wake up to what is going on.

Subtle bullying

What most teachers at reputable music colleges have in common is the importance they place on high standards, and this is as it should be. It is demanding to become a professional musician and you need to be well qualified in the mastery of music and your instrument.

The bullying I have mentioned so far is extreme and unacceptable, but working under pressure towards high standards can be very *subtly* dangerous. It can be insidious and go unnoticed, but it often involves repeated criticism without the reassuring recognition or encouragement that is needed. It is not the high standards themselves; it is when they come at the cost of the student.

When Sergei left his home in Eastern Europe at the age of sixteen, he studied with a teacher who was considered one of the best around. He was talented and enthusiastic, but his teacher was frustrated because he was not quite up to the standard that she was used to.

She complained about him on a weekly basis for not being 'good enough', never recognising the work he had put in or giving him any encouragement.

This is a form of bullying, but it is often not seen in this way. The teacher was considered good and she demanded high standards, so the behaviour was deemed acceptable and normal. And yet Sergei was not learning and improving as he was so keen to do; his response to his increasing distress was shooting pains in his arms.

It can be more subtle still. For example, a teacher might ask his student *"Why* haven't you learnt this from memory?" in a tone that implies disapproval. It could easily make the student feel uncomfortable, and yet the teacher feels that the demand for high standards justifies the criticism.

- *Are there teachers, conductors or section principals you have felt uncomfortable with?*
- *Do these stories resonate because you have had similar experiences?*
- *Can you identify times when you felt bullied?*

The impact of bullying

How does this kind of treatment affect a musician? The most obvious is confidence. It is very difficult to keep a healthy amount of confidence and self-belief, if you have been repeatedly told you are no good. It chips away at any confidence you have, and that has its own consequences.

You start seeing the world through very negative filters. You don't believe you are good enough, you don't believe you stand a chance with various goals, such as exams or competitions.

You start attracting failure because that is how you see yourself.

That then perpetuates your feelings that you aren't good enough. It might lead you to giving up when you otherwise might not have done.

Bullying also has a massive impact on *learning*. When you are being treated in this way, you are in survival mode, doing whatever it takes to cope with the situation. This is not conducive to learning.

To learn effectively you need to be open, free, receptive and supported.

Enjoyment, fun and laughter are vital for learning. Think how a young child learns through play. You need to know that you are capable and that with the right guidance you can develop mastery. You need someone to believe in you so that you can then believe in yourself. Bullying can create wounds which may go very deep if they are not addressed, and the effects last for years. This was the case with John.

A lengthy wound

John was in his late fifties when he decided to start playing the piano again for pleasure and enjoyment. On one occasion, we were trying out different aspects of memorising. I gave him a very simple exercise and asked him to memorise two bars. He had a complete mental block and couldn't remember a single note. Just minutes before, he had played very well, so it was surprising to see him suddenly so lacking in confidence. He froze at the piano, paralysed by fear. He tried again and again to get it right, refusing to give up. He was in so much discomfort and it was painful to watch him struggle in this way. I asked him whether he had any sense of why he was reacting like this. He told me that he had had a teacher when he was a child who had insisted he memorised everything. If he made a mistake, the teacher would hit his hands with a ruler. John still had the emotional scars from those lessons five decades on.

- *What emotional events, good or bad, have impacted your playing? Are there areas you feel anxious about?*
- *Can you pinpoint a moment or person that crystallised this for you?*
- *In what way have they affected you as a musician?*

It is not personal

If you have ever been treated like this, rest assured that this is nothing to do with you. It might feel like it, but it really isn't. It is not personal.

Teachers are under pressure too.

They might feel that they have to get 'perfection' out of their students to be seen as a good teacher; they may have pressure from their superiors, from the college. Someone who lashes out, makes snide comments, raises their voice, has their own unresolved emotional issues, and are taking their unconscious pain out on you. They are unlikely to be conscious of how their actions are impacting you. It feels normal to them.

That teacher may have received the same treatment from their teachers. They may have received the same tough demands, the same bullying actions, and they are simply perpetuating the cycle. It goes on for generation after generation until there are people who say "Enough is enough. It doesn't have to continue!"

It is not helpful to blame the person who has given you such a tough time. Blaming doesn't achieve anything. Nor can you wish they would change so that you can feel better. That is up to them.

Taking back your power

The most empowering thing you can do is to take full responsibility for how you feel, and make your own choices as a result of that.

Joseph came from a small town in Africa to study at music college in the UK. He couldn't understand why he was been treated with such negativity by his teacher, and because it was so far removed from his own understanding and experience, he thought it must be some strange form of British humour. He put up with it for almost two years, thinking it must be normal because that was what he was seeing all around him. But he was also aware he was changing, and not for the better. His vitality and self-esteem were being destroyed bit by bit over time. He was not the same vibrant, fun-loving man who had arrived in the UK two years earlier.

He came across an incident that was the last straw for him. He witnessed his teacher throwing music at the student who was having the lesson before him, shouting at her that she was no good. She left in tears, distraught. Joseph had a flash of insight and realised he had to do something, simply for the sake of his own self-preservation. He told his teacher on the spot that he was stopping lessons. Within an hour, the head of department was on the phone asking him to reconsider, but Joseph had had enough. He not only left the teacher, but he also left the college.

You can choose to let the bullying continue, you can choose to rise above it and get a bigger perspective using some of the techniques above, or you can do something more extreme. You can leave. Leaving can be a challenge, because it may be that you need to go against the status quo. If everyone still holds the teacher up on a pedestal, then you may get some opposition to what the majority thinks, and that can be difficult.

Joseph made a courageous decision that came from a sense of self-preservation. By refusing to be a victim to the circumstances, he took his power back into his own hands and was able to regain his self-esteem and confidence. It was an extreme choice, but sometimes an extreme choice is what is necessary. You have to look after yourself.

It is very easy to give your power away, especially to people who are your teachers and guides, and who you would expect to have your own best interests at heart.

By taking your power back into your own hands, you don't give it away to the perpetrator. This is fundamentally the most important thing you can do. Your choices come from this.

- *If you have ever felt bullied, were you able to feel the pressures that your bully might be under?*
- *How could you go about trying not take this personally and let go of blaming?*
- *How can you start taking responsibility for your own feelings and choices?*
- *At what point do you assess the damage and ask if it's all worth it? Are you willing to carry on regardless? Or have you really had enough?*

Summary

If you have had experience of bullying, you don't need to be a victim of it; you do have choices.

- **The first step** is becoming aware of what is going on and realising that you don't need to put up with it.

- **The second step** is realising that bullying is not personal. Just knowing that the perpetrator is unconsciously repeating their own pain can take the pressure off.

- **The third step** is to take responsibility for what you feel about the situation. This means that you let go of blaming and you find ways to deal with it that work for you.

The impact that bullying can have on a musician can be brutal or subtle, and if you have suffered in the past, you may feel inspired to take control and reclaim the power that you once gave away.

In Chapter 3 we will meet another destructive bully: the Inner Critic.

3

The Inner Critic

Take the Bully from the last chapter, turn it inwards, bed it down and there you have it: the Inner Critic! This is the nasty, destructive way it shows up in the head of someone who is run by their Inner Critic:

"I'm such a **** idiot... That was pathetic... I can't believe I played that so badly... There's no point in doing that again... It'll never get any better!"

The Inner Critic is the sum of everything negative that you have heard from outside about yourself and that you have chosen to believe and take on board.

The Inner Critic does not offer you objective, dispassionate criticism. It is very personal and always negative. It has a tendency towards victimhood, is very disempowering and does not lend itself to free, expressive playing. It loves perfectionism because it is unattainable, and this means that it can always be critical of the inevitable failure that results. It does not have your best interests at heart.

The Inner Critic can be the most damaging part of your journey towards excellent playing. What makes it even more damaging is that it is so covert. It doesn't want you to see the games it is up to.

It wants to win by losing, by bringing you down.

It wants you to blame everyone and everything else, rather than take responsibility for changing its behaviour. And yet that is what you need to do, if you are going to be the best musician you can be.

The Inner Critic versus the Objective Observer

Imagine that you slipped up in a particular passage and that you played a G instead of an F#. The Inner Critic would say: "Oh God, I'm such an idiot... I messed up... It's supposed to be an F# not a G... Oh, get it right this time you jerk!" If the Inner Critic is really firmly engrained, it might say: "Oh not again... Not the same mistake... I'm such a hopeless player... No one will ever book me if I play like that..." But it was only a G instead of an F#!

Criticism definitely has its place. In order to learn, improve your skills and play well, you need to be critical, but you need to be *objective* in your criticism. You need to discern what needs improving and what you need to do about it without any emotional involvement. This is where the Objective Observer comes in.

The Objective Observer would say something totally different. "Oops, that was a G instead of an F#. Why did I do that? Oh – I need a better fingering – good, that's better." Observing what is needed is enough. It is unemotional and therefore kinder. It keeps you free and open, ready to learn and improve. Negative emotional involvement just gets in the way.

What is important here is to notice the difference in language between the Inner Critic and the Objective Observer.

The Inner Critic is cruel and unkind. It can even be vicious.
The Objective Observer is much kinder.

"Oops, I slipped up" is more forgiving, lighter in tone and can even prompt a laugh. The Inner Critic is the culmination of negative thoughts that get stuck and become a bad habit. The good news is that bad habits can be changed.

There is another key difference between the Inner Critic and the Objective Observer. The Inner Critic assumes the worst – "This has gone wrong therefore I am bad" – and the Objective Observer assumes the best: "I know that I can do this, I just need to learn how and give myself the best chance." This is very important. You will no doubt have had experiences of working with conductors or musical directors who don't have an entirely positive approach. Even though nothing may be said, you feel that they don't believe in you, that you automatically *can't* play well. The result is that you don't play at your best and might end up being angry and resentful to boot. Your Inner Critic will have a field day. You will feel completely justified to beat yourself up again because that person also 'implied' through a negative approach that you were no good.

When someone comes along who completely believes in you, assumes the
best and trusts that you can do it, you rise to the occasion and play well.

You are far more likely to enjoy the experience too! Lack of confidence and self-belief is one of the key manifestations of the Inner Critic, as we will see with Jon.

The Inner Critic consumes self-belief

Jon came for lessons with great enthusiasm, loved the piano and was keen to improve. He practised well and yet whenever he felt he played badly, he would go into a cold, silent rage. He would turn pale, wouldn't hear anything I said and was consumed by what he perceived as his own inadequacy. He couldn't think straight, his arms tightened and playing well and expressively was out of the question.

What he was saying in his head was undoubtedly furious and negative, and probably aimed at himself.

I could see that Jon was totally in the clutches of his Inner Critic and I knew that what he needed more than anything else at that moment were two things: perspective and kindness. He was so involved in the intensity of his feelings that he couldn't see out, and didn't know how to get himself out. I reminded him of how much he had improved in the few years since he had been coming for lessons.

He began to see that whatever he felt about himself at that moment was just a blip in the bigger picture.

I picked out incidents in which he had excelled himself and reminded him how he had managed to get back on track before. And then I encouraged him to be kind to himself. I had to be the role model for this first so that it was easier for him to get there from a place of such intense negative emotions. After about half an hour, he gradually calmed, started to breathe more deeply and his arms freed up. It was one more step along the journey of transforming the Inner Critic.

A lack of self-belief has an insidious way of winding itself into your unconscious. When it is deeply ingrained, it starts having an impact on the filters through which you see the world. I noticed this early on with Claire.

Claire was constantly telling me that she couldn't play well and that she wasn't going to give a good recital. She would even question why she was playing the piano. She convinced herself that she was no good, to the extent that her inner filters filtered out any positive feedback she was given. She couldn't hear it and only had ears for the negatives that proved her story of herself was right.

So it became a self-fulfilling prophecy and the world started reflecting back to her exactly what she didn't want.

She would come to me and say, "See, I wasn't given that recital opportunity. That shows they think I'm rubbish." She would then go into destructive self-blame and the vicious cycle would continue. I spent a lot of time talking to her about the power of her Inner Critic, showing her what she was doing to herself. It wasn't easy; she was very resistant and fought me every step of the way.

When you are in the grip of the Inner Critic you are in a very disempowered state. You are being run like a puppet from a part of you that wants to keep you in the drama and keep you stuck. Jon's rage at himself was so strong that he couldn't hear anything that would support him. He was stopping himself from playing at a high standard with freedom and expression. Claire was so stubborn with her story that nothing I or anybody else could say would shift it. My words bounced back to me unheard. There was no room for them. She was creating walls around her where no one could help. The only person who could help her was herself.

- *In what ways are you in the grip of the Inner Critic?*
- *How does it show?*
- *How could you talk more kindly to yourself and get things in perspective?*

The terrible fear of making mistakes

In the last chapter, I mentioned perfectionism and how it is all around us in our society. Hand in hand with perfectionism comes the fear of making mistakes. A very young child will naturally play, automatically 'making mistakes' as a part of that play, but never thinking that they are mistakes.

Young children don't judge themselves. To them it is just play, which is their way of learning about the world. But something changes en route and a moral judgement comes into play.

They realise that learning about the world now involves either making mistakes or not making mistakes. Making mistakes is considered a 'bad' thing, whereas not making mistakes or getting something 'right,' is considered a 'good' thing. They discover that doing something 'right' brings them praise, and making mistakes, doing something 'wrong', brings them disapproval and even punishment. So naturally, they want to get things 'right' and avoid the mistakes.

Making mistakes is a learned, conditioned behaviour; and yet mistakes are an integral part of learning. As the great jazz trumpeter Miles Davis said, "Don't fear mistakes, there are none."

Mistakes are your biggest resource because they show you what doesn't work, so that you then have a clearer idea of what does work.

The child at play has got it right. Left to their own devices they would have a healthy approach to learning. But the judgement around making mistakes is deeply lodged in our collective psyches. It can be difficult to let go.

Alicia and the panic-ometer

Alicia was a pianist as well as a brilliant academic. During one lesson, she was having problems playing a trill. She needed to understand how to play it rhythmically and then with a freedom in her hands. I explained a number of times and she gave me the impression that she had understood, only to find that her hands became 'jammed up' with tension. It didn't make sense to me at first. She was intelligent, she was capable and she was willing, but try as she would, she couldn't play this particular ornament.

I then realised that she was panicking. We talked a little about it and it became clear that she had spent her entire life attempting to perform to a level of perfection at enormous cost to herself. She would work through the night if necessary and would get very distressed if she didn't reach the level she felt she should reach. Once we had identified the panic hidden away in a seemingly innocuous ornament, we had something to go on. I set her what I called a 'panic-ometer'. Whenever she showed signs of panic at not being able to play the ornament, she would give me levels out of ten. Ten was the highest level of panic, with zero being none at all. She focused on bringing it down step by step, starting at eight and eventually going down to zero, needing enormous amounts of reassurance for it to go down even one step.

This was a powerful exercise because it showed me how deeply engrained these belief systems can be and how the essential qualities needed to shift beyond them are kindness and reassurance. It would have been difficult for Alicia to have moved down the scale if she hadn't felt safe, and it was my role to support her in that.

For Alicia, the panic-ometer was enlightening because it increased her awareness of feelings that she didn't know she had.

By bringing these feelings to the surface, she had allowed herself the first steps towards letting go and retraining.

The fear of making mistakes acts as a strait jacket. It limits and restricts you and your body tenses up. You need to feel safe to make those mistakes as a natural part of learning, not as a sign that you are not up to the mark and are failing in some way. You can't be wearing a strait jacket when you are performing because you won't be expressing yourself at your peak. You will be just coping, mentally and physically, getting through the performance somehow, rather than having the freedom to let the performance come alive.

A fear of making mistakes can also put you in the role of trying to please others. Your energy goes into getting things right for the sake of the people around you, and you try to match *their* standards and *their* ideals.

Your body locks out of fear of not getting things right to impress or please someone else.

33

You can become so wrapped up in trying to please other people that you lose contact with who you are, what you want to do, and you stop listening to yourself. This is another way of giving away your power to other people and the Inner Critic is expert at helping you do this. After all, you're no good anyway so you have to defer to other people. They are of course better than you are.

Edison's reply to a journalist, when he was asked how he felt about his constant failures to invent the light bulb, was that he didn't consider any to be failures, and that he was pleased now that he knew all the different ways *not* to invent a light bulb. His success lay in his willingness to make mistakes and learn from them in order to achieve his goal.

Perfectionism: the Inner Critic's partner in crime

All around us in modern day society, we see attempts at perfection. CDs are made with hundreds of takes and thoroughly edited, enabling little slips and blemishes to be ironed out. They promote false standards that are impossible to live up to. But perfectionism is in fact a bully. It can demand more of a musician than is possible.

The danger of perfectionism is that you feel restricted by it, locked into the need to 'get it all right'. It is a pressure that forces you to become overly worried by that demand, meaning you can end up disregarding your own desire to let go and express yourself freely through the music. If you play every note perfectly in place with no mistakes, that is an achievement, but that is all it is. A performance needs more than notes in the right place: it needs interpretation and expression.

There is no such thing as a perfect means of expression or interpretation, because what one person considers perfect is not perfect by someone else's standards. Whilst high standards are laudable, if we see perfection as a kind of bully, we can reduce its impact and by doing so help to make room for true, joyful expression.

The pressure of perfectionism

From the culture of perfectionism comes pressure. There is so much pressure in the music profession today. "You are only as good as your last concert" is what is commonly said.

It is all too easy to push yourself beyond what is actually manageable because you fear not getting through an audition, losing concerts and losing opportunities.

But ironically this is more likely to happen if you keep yourself under constant pressure. Too much pressure leads to getting ill or burnt out. I was once told about a French horn player who had been suffering under the intense pressure that can come along with being a professional musician. He got to the end of his tether and threw his French horn under a steam roller! Laurel and Hardy did the same, but not for the same reasons! It is much better to learn to say no when you need to.

- *Are you aware of any external pressures such as perfectionism that could be negatively affecting you?*

Seeing the bigger picture

Pressure can result in being buried in a small perspective when what you need is to look at the big picture.

I was once coaching a student for his final recital. Mike was practising for hours a day but his recital programme wasn't getting any better.

He was so wrapped up in his recital that it was as if his whole life depended on it.

I knew that if he continued in this way of thinking, he wouldn't give a good performance. So I worked with him on shifting his perspective. I got him to think way into the future and imagine himself at the age of 40 or 50, looking back at himself at the age of 21, in the days leading up to his final recital. What would his future self say? Would his future self think that it was as important or significant as his present self was thinking it was?

With these new considerations, he realised that his recital wasn't as all encompassing as he had thought it was. He was able to shift into a broader perspective and let go of the pressure. As a result, he eased up on his incessant, inefficient practising, doing only what was necessary to make a difference. He took the weekend off, went out with his friends and had fun.

He sent me a text that weekend saying that he was feeling great and was actually looking forward to his recital. A few days later, he walked onto the concert platform a different person, and played better than I had ever heard him play. All the practising in the world wouldn't have got him to that place. He had to change his thinking and take the pressure off. And it was a wonderful bonus when he rang me to tell me he had got a First!

The 'F**k it' switch

I first discovered this delightfully irreverent technique through two colleagues who were using it on a regular basis. I now do the same. It is a great way of taking the stress off in the moment and freeing yourself up; it is a wonderful antidote to an overdose of perfectionism!

When everything gets too much and you find yourself getting overly wound up in the spur of the moment, you can employ the 'F**k it switch'. It is as simple as saying 'F**k it!', which is another way of saying 'Let it go. What does it all matter? Life's too short!' It can be used from anything as seemingly insignificant as a violinist approaching a difficult shift, to managing the stress around a Wigmore Hall recital. The 'F**k it' switch resets the balance and gets you back into the big picture again. Try it when you are worried about a particular passage. Let go and let live! You will start finding a new freedom in your playing.

See the funny side

Laughter can be just as effective in shifting back into a bigger perspective. Seeing the lighter side of a pressurised situation can work magic. It is so easy to become overly serious when with the flick of a switch – the 'F**k it' switch or the laughter switch – you can shift into a lighter, brighter perspective.

- *How could you take the pressure off yourself whilst still playing to high standards?*
- *How could you shift to a broader perspective to alleviate pressure?*
- *In what ways could you use humour to alleviate stressful situations?*

The difference between perfection and excellence

I agree whole-heartedly with playing to the highest of standards. What is important to me is how these high standards are reached. Criticism and bullying in their various guises have always been accepted forms of achieving high standards, but we have already seen how damaging these can be.

I've come to realise that people often see perfection as being the same as excellence, and that the end justifies the means. I see them as two distinct things; one is damaging and the other much healthier:

Perfection is impossible	**Excellence** is always possible
Perfection is working towards an ideal that can never be reached. It is unattainable. It is driving yourself towards that goal and never being satisfied.	**Excellence** is working towards your own personal best, aiming at the highest standards you are capable of, with flexibility and freedom. It is about enjoying the process of practising and performing and gaining deep fulfilment from the experience for its own sake.
Perfection works with the Inner Critic and the Bully as constant companions.	**Excellence** works with the Objective Observer.
Perfection is unforgiving. Mistakes are 'bad'.	**Excellence** recognises that you can make mistakes to achieve the high standards you are aiming for.

Perfection demands perfection at any cost.	**Excellence** acknowledges that you can never meet ideals of perfection, whatever they might be, and is comfortable with that.
Perfection demands constant striving. It doesn't matter if you don't feel good. You can never let yourself off the hook.	**Excellence** accepts that you are fallible. It is ok to have down days when you don't feel at your best and you are not playing at your best. It knows that being fallible is essential for your emotional well-being and your playing.
Perfection doesn't care what you do or what you feel, as long as you produce a perfect result.	**Excellence** recognises that playing at your best needs openness, receptivity, curiosity, fascination and a willingness to get it wrong, in order to find the best way to do it.
Perfection uses bullying or even cruelty to get results.	**Excellence** recognises that kindness is essential to reach high standards. Kindness allows space, openness and the freedom to truly express yourself.

- *Are you on the side of perfection or excellence?*
- *How does this reveal itself in the way you treat yourself?*
- *Can you think of a time when you allowed yourself to make a mistake, learned from it and achieved a better result?*

The physical impact of the Inner Critic

Your fear of making mistakes and your judgement of them can have a surprising impact on your progress and how you play. The most obvious way is through physical tightening. You just have to imagine playing in front of someone who you know is going to pull your playing apart and you will find yourself tensing up.

> *Then remember that the Inner Critic is your own built-in version of the outer bully, and you don't need someone else to find fault with you in order to tense up.*

You can very successfully do that on your own!

Joanne was having some difficulties playing a certain demanding passage on the piano. It was clear to me that her wrist was locked and that this was partly to blame. I showed her how to find a freedom in her wrist by doing an exercise in which she allowed her wrist to be entirely flexible, moving freely up and down, whilst depressing her fingers on the keys of the piano. She understood on an intellectual level what I was asking, but much as she wanted to let go, she couldn't seem to get her hands to co-operate. Her wrist went through a series of miniscule jolts and jerks, as if she was relaxing and then immediately tightening up again. I then got her to do the same exercise on her thigh, so that she was away from the keyboard entirely. This time she managed it.

At the keyboard she could only manage small jerky movements. I asked her what the difference was between doing it on her thigh and doing it on the keyboard, and she said that when she took her hand away from the keyboard she was free from associations. As soon as she put her hands on the keys, the Inner Critic took hold and lots of fears and anxieties loomed in her mind. She said, "You see, I just can't get it wrong – after all, my whole career depends on getting it right!"

Tensing up is a way of bracing yourself for protection under the real or imagined threat of attack. If the perceived attack is low lying, on-going and ever present in the form of judgement, then the bracing will be the same. This tightening up mostly comes in small, barely noticeable ways. Your Inner Critic projects outwards that this person is going to have a negative response to you and you brace yourself in anticipation. It might come before you do something technically demanding, when the nagging voice of your Inner Critic tells you that you can't do it. This tension mostly hides itself very successfully and becomes an inability to play fast passagework or to play accurately and fluently.

When you tighten up in small ways like this on a regular basis, it can accumulate and become one big tightening up.

This invariably leads to strain and difficulties playing, resulting in the physical dysfunctions no musician wants – tendonitis, problems with embouchure, and in the case of singers, nodules on the vocal cords.

The mask of arrogance

The Inner Critic is subtle and manipulative, and can show up in ways that you would never associate with inner criticism. I've come across people who have an inflated opinion of themselves, making it clear to anyone around them who will listen that they are wonderful, talented and the top of the bunch. Generally, the people who have to tell everyone how good they are have quite a low opinion of themselves underneath the 'confident' exterior. It is the Inner Critic in disguise. The Inner Critic takes all those negative feelings and wraps them up in a cloak of arrogance.

Arrogance is a disaster on the concert platform. It acts as a mask. The musician becomes the mask and they perform to impress and not to inspire.

It stops them from exposing their true self through the music.

It is very often these same people who act as if everyone else is no good and worthless, and not as good as they are. They take their own Inner Critic and instead of beating themselves up, they project it outwards onto other people. Their Inner Critic becomes an Outer Critic and they risk becoming the Bully of the last chapter, to hide their own feelings of not being good enough.

They criticise other people. It is their way of surviving, putting other people down in order to make themselves feel better.

They resent the opportunities other people are given, resent their success and attack them behind their back. It is a game, and it is a very cruel game. What they are not recognising is that the other people out there are just like them. They, too, are dealing with their own Inner Critic and they don't need any more criticism from outside. Once those people see that, they can choose to start being supportive. And then they discover, to their amazement, that support comes flooding back.

- *Have you ever recognised the need to put on a mask in order to impress? Have you ever felt that mask stopped you from showing the real you?*

- *Have you ever sensed that exposing your vulnerability through music can speak for itself, and that you may not need the mask?*
- *Have you ever felt tempted to criticise other people in order to make yourself feel better?*

Summary

If you have become best friends with your Inner Critic, this is the time to take a long hard look at what's going on.

- **The first step** is to hear the Inner Critic and make the decision not to be driven by it.

- **The second step** is to shift your thoughts from negative criticism into the kinder, less emotionally involved Objective Observer.

- **The third step** is to become comfortable with making mistakes and be able to see their value.

- **The fourth step** is to be aware that you can reach standards of excellence without allowing perfectionism to drive you into the ground.

You will never totally do away with the Inner Critic; you have to use it as a starting point but know how to transform it so that it can become your ally.

In Chapter 4 we will see the different ways in which you can transform the Inner Critic.

4

Transform your Inner Critic

The only way to make sense out of change is to plunge into it, move with it, and join the dance.
Alan Watts

The Inner Critic is dangerous and has far-reaching consequences that can impact your life. You may not even be aware of what you are doing. Put it this way: think of a very young child who is at the early stages of learning to walk. He takes a few steps, falters and falls down. Then he gets himself up, takes a few more steps, wobbles, takes a few more steps and falls down again. Now think of the child's mother and how she would react. She would be delighted, thrilled and totally absorbed by her child's first stumbling attempts at walking and would encourage him, smiling. She wouldn't say to him: "You stupid child... I can't believe you've fallen over again... You're so useless... Get up and do it again – and get it right this time!"

Now think about what you allow your Inner Critic to get away with. How often have you spoken like this to yourself when you have been practising or when you have come off the concert platform at the end of a concert?

Would you do this to a very young child? If the answer is no, think very carefully about why you would do it to yourself.

The Inner Critic becomes so engrained that we depend on it, justifying it to ourselves by saying we need it to "keep us on our toes". It's hard to make the Inner Critic redundant, but with support we can move on and experience an amazing transformation. This was the case with Valentina.

Valentina's transformational journey

Valentina came to me having had a ten-year break from the piano. She was a classic case of a student who had been badly bullied. Brought up in Eastern Europe and taught by a strict aunt from the age of six to fifteen, she was made to do long hours of practice from a very young age with no concern about whether she wanted to or not. Valentina never had a choice in what she did, and always felt she had to fit into other people's agenda for her. It was during these intense years of learning the piano that she internalised the voice of her aunt, which turned into her Inner Critic. At the age of fifteen, however, she snapped and refused to play the piano anymore.

At 25, she was both overjoyed at being back at the piano again and absolutely terrified. Her arms were rigid, her breath was locked and the tension in her body was so great that she could hardly play a line of music, let alone a whole piece.

She didn't know who she was in relation to the piano and needed to embark on a voyage of self-discovery.

It became clear to her that in order to play the piano well again, she needed to change on a very big scale. It was a case of letting go of her old ways of doing things, her old ways of talking to herself, moving out of her comfort zone and into her 'risk' zone. She needed to make an internal paradigm shift.

I encouraged her to bring 'play' back into her playing, the imaginative play that is so natural for a young child. She needed to regain the sense of wonder, fun and spontaneity that she had lost.

By being given space and by not being judged, she started feeling safe enough to free up. Bit by bit the tension eased, her breath flowed more and she noticed how much easier it was to play.

She loved her new-found freedom, and yet she went back again and again to her previous habits of tense arms and locked breath. It was scary and new for Valentina, and she started to sabotage her progress to keep in line with what had previously been so familiar.

One week she was ten minutes late for the lesson because she had shut her hand in a door, as she was leaving. It wasn't bad enough to damage it, but enough to give her a shock and make her late. There was an unconscious part of her that didn't want to come, despite the rest of her that was loving her lessons. She laughed when she told the story and said that she had imagined that it was her aunt trying to get her to stop coming!

Valentina told me that she felt very scared when she was practising because all the change felt too overwhelming. It felt like being a frightened child plucking up the courage to go back into her own bedroom after a nightmare.

She acknowledged that her mind wanted to move on but that her emotions and her body were reacting and were scared.

"Phew! Now I can go back to a safe place," she said with a smile at the end of one lesson. "This all feels a bit too dangerous!"

She started to enjoy the lessons more and more, feeling increasingly comfortable, but still she felt her aunt was looking over her shoulder criticising what she was doing. "My aunt doesn't like this. She thinks this way of doing things is stupid," she said in one lesson, showing how much the voice of her aunt had become one and the same, along with her own Inner Critic. We laughed because what I was showing Valentina would have been so utterly different from what she would have been taught as a child. The laughter was a relief and freeing and I knew that she was well on track in her own personal process of change.

Valentina's experience shows that the journey of change doesn't follow a linear route. You take a risk to move out of your comfort zone; you go backwards and forwards, learning the new ways, forgetting, going back to the old ways, sabotaging, moving on to the new ways and getting confused between the two. And then one day you find that you can't even remember the old way anymore.

Once Valentina knew that she wasn't going to be judged, she could dare to be herself. She freed up physically and emotionally and with this freedom, she took the courageous step of showing her vulnerability in her playing. Her true self, her expressive self, was now really shining through and her playing became vital and alive.

She played in a way that would one minute lift me and inspire me and the next move me to tears.

The journey of transformation may be full of challenges, but the benefits are unsurpassed.

Transformation: what does it mean?

Imagine you are an actor with a small role in a play you know well. To your horror, you have just been fired from the play and have been promised a starring role in a much more satisfying play – better written, better supporting actors and exactly what you have always hoped for. But you have been very comfortable in the play that you are in. You like your small role, you know your script inside out and back to front, you know all the actors very well and it is all very familiar. Moving to a new play means a new script to learn and become familiar with, new actors to get to know and much more responsibility in the new, bigger role. You are filled with doubts and questions. Will it really be much better than I have now? How can I guarantee that it will be better? What happens if it doesn't work out?

Change can be scary. It can feel as if you are jumping off a cliff without a parachute. On some deep level you are not sure whether you will survive it.

You are leaving your comfort zone and moving into a risk zone. Your comfort zone is actually not comfortable at all, so I am going to change the word to familiar, because familiar it certainly is. The risk zone is where you grow, and it can take courage to grow.

- *Have you been using the Inner Critic as a way of "keeping yourself on your toes"?*
- *Have you had enough of carrying the Inner Critic on your back?*
- *Are you ready to move on to a freer, healthier, happier way of performing?*

If you have really had enough, you will have the momentum to move forwards.

Imagine a footpath across a field. It is very long and windy and very inefficient, taking you far too long to get to the other side of the field. But it is very visible and well worn, so it is much easier to go down that path. There is an alternative. There is a new path that goes straight across the field but this path is not at all well worn and it is not always easy seeing that it is a path at all. You start going on the new path, but the old, well-worn path is still easier. With lots of walking on the new path, this starts to become the well-worn path, and the big advantage is that it is a far better path.

Transformation of the Inner Critic is all about reprogramming yourself. Understanding where you have been and where you want to move to is only the first step.

You need to build in a very different approach from what hasn't worked for you before so that it becomes a dominant part of your behaviour.

You are changing your neurology, creating new neural pathways and then consolidating the new pathways with lots of repetition. It is creating a new, better habit.

Tools of transformation

Here are three tools that are very simple and yet extremely powerful.

Jay and Terry Brightwater, two exceptionally gifted life coaches with whom I have had the privilege of working, taught me these wonderful tools and they in turn learnt them from William Bloom. These tools have had an incredible impact on me and I have used them time and time again. If you do nothing else from this book, do these! They really are transformational.

Pause, Breathe, Kind Eyes

Whenever you recognise the Inner Critic in action:

- *Pause:* this gives you time and space to observe what is happening, without judgement.
- *Breathe:* this gets the oxygen moving round your system and calms down an overactive nervous system.
- *Kind Eyes:* look at yourself with kindness. It is like a small child who is really distressed by falling over and grazing his knee and whose mother just takes him and hugs him quietly. The child feels the love and kindness, and when he has had his fill, can run off again and play with his friends again. This is what you do for yourself.

It is so simple but this tool has far-reaching effects. Catch yourself whenever you are beating yourself up and try it out. Don't worry if you find that you manage the first two but that you struggle with the Kind Eyes. It may well be very unfamiliar to be kind to yourself. You might hope for it from other people, but doing it for yourself is not what you are used to. And yet, once you start building that kindness for yourself, it tends to increase from outside too.

Be kind to yourself when you are making mistakes and showing your fallibility; be kind to yourself when you are beating yourself up for making those mistakes; be kind to yourself when you don't feel you are doing very well at changing your Inner Critic! Kindness has enormous power.

"Be kind whenever possible. It is always possible." – the Dalai Lama.

Open language versus closed language

Another useful technique is changing the language you use with yourself from 'closed' to 'open'.

Imagine you have been very self-critical and you don't know what to do to move yourself out of the clutches of your Inner Critic. You have just said to yourself: "I can't play this passage", and you have feeling really bad about it. Saying "I can't play this passage" is closed and shut down. There is no space for the possibility that you *could* play it well.

But you have caught yourself being negative and you know that this is not helping you at all, so you decide to say something that is neither down on yourself nor upbeat. It is half way between, open and with possibilities. You say instead, "I *wonder* if I can play this passage" or "what would it be like if I could play this really well?"

By saying "I wonder... What if... Maybe I can...", you move into a place of openness and expectancy.

This 'half-way' idea is much easier to reach from a place of doom and gloom, and it is then much easier to find yourself beginning to feel more upbeat.

Here are some examples of things you might say to yourself:

Closed: "I'm playing really badly... This will never sound good."	**Open:** "I wonder what I need to do to get this to sound better."
Closed: "I'm exhausted... I'm not achieving enough."	**Open:** "What if I take a break now? I might find it easier to concentrate."
Closed: "I've got so much to do – I'm never going to get this memorised in time."	**Open:** "Wouldn't it be great if I could memorise this? Maybe if I give myself more time, I'll find it easier."
Closed: "I am never going to manage that concert – I just don't know the music well enough."	**Open:** "I wonder whether I can play really well in that concert. What if I could learn that music really well?"

- *Have you noticed the language you use?*
- *How do you feel when you use open language compared to closed language?*
- *How can you lessen the grip of the Inner Critic through the language you use?*

If you are feeling low and despondent, your self-esteem is at an all time low and you can't think how you can ever perform successfully in the concert next week, you know that it doesn't help to be told by someone very well meaning to "cheer up". Moving into the positive "can do" mentality might feel like climbing Mount Everest. Every time you try, you slide down back into despondency again. But rather than trying the emotional version of trying to climb Mount Everest, you can do something much more manageable, something that is just a little bit more positive. This is where the Emotional Guidance System comes in.

Finding better feelings through the Emotional Guidance System

The Emotional Guidance System is another astonishingly powerful tool which comes from the book *'Ask and It is Given'* by Esther and Jerry Hicks. It ranks feelings in a kind of ladder, with Fear at the bottom and Love at the top, and the Emotional Guidance System helps you to inch your way up the ladder from feeling bad to feeling good.

The "ladder" of emotions and how to use it

Joy / Knowledge / Empowerment / Freedom / Love / Appreciation

Passion

Enthusiasm / Eagerness / Happiness

Positive Expectation / Belief

Optimism

Hopefulness

Contentment

Boredom

Pessimism

Frustration / Irritation / Impatience

Overwhelm

Disappointment

Doubt

Worry

Blame

Discouragement

Anger

Revenge

Hatred / Rage / Jealousy

Insecurity / Guilt / Unworthiness

Fear / Grief / Depression / Despair / Powerlessness

If you are feeling depressed, for example, it can actually be a relief to move up to anger, by transforming your thoughts. There is more energy in anger than there is in depression; anger is good in that it can spur you on to take action, and it moves you on from feeling really bad to feeling a bit better. Just going up the ladder by one step is an improvement, and much more manageable than expecting yourself to feel fantastic straight away.

Obviously you don't want to stay stuck in angry feelings for too long, so once they no longer feel like an improvement, you would use them as a platform to move up the ladder to a feeling of frustration, perhaps, which still gives to you the energy to solve the problem but takes the heat out of your thoughts.

- *Have you been able to catch yourself feeling bad about your playing?*
- *If so, how have you managed to shift 'up the ladder' to a better feeling?*
- *What difference did you notice?*

Summary

If you are in the grip of the Inner Critic and want to be free, this is what you can do:

- **The first step** is to be aware that you're never stuck with the Inner Critic. It's always possible to transform it.

- **The second step** is to use any of the techniques we have looked at to shift the negative voice to one that is kinder, more positive and supportive to yourself.

- **The third step** is to make a real point of noticing which of the techniques really works for you and using them consistently every time your Inner Critic attacks. Do what it takes again and again and notice the power you are gaining.

We've done some very profound work in this chapter. The Inner Critic is a stubborn customer, but to be free of it will enable you to get so much more enjoyment from the music.

In Chapter 5 we move on to tackle the greatest enemy of performing on stage: Nerves.

5

Manage your nerves

> *I remember being on stage once when I didn't have fear: I got so scared I didn't have fear that it brought on an anxiety attack.*
> **Carly Simon**

Backstage at the Royal Festival Hall, and one of the symphony orchestras is preparing to go on stage to give a concert. People are tuning up, putting resin on their bows, warming up their instruments. It seems totally normal and you would almost think that everyone was so professional and so used to giving concerts that they didn't suffer from nerves at all. But the reality is different.

Chris is silently going over his flute solo in his mind, his heart beating wildly and his breathing short and sharp. Despite his professionalism and his years of experience, he is terrified and barely slept the night before.

Lucy is wiping her hands on a tissue; she has been leading the cellos for six years now and still has clammy fingers before she goes on stage. She can't risk her fingers sliding on the fingerboard so she wipes her hands constantly in preparation. Dave, first horn, split a note in one of the most exposed and difficult solos in the repertoire a few years ago, and nearly died on the spot. Ever since then, he has had such crippling nerves that he takes no risks and always resorts to beta-blockers. Naomi, one of the second violins, doesn't feel quite so pressurised because she is surrounded by other players and never plays solos, but try as she might, she always ends up chatting incessantly and nervously about anything at all just before she goes on stage. It is her way of releasing excess nervous energy. Anita, a viola player, feels heavy and tired before she goes on stage and then becomes alert as soon as she starts to play. It doesn't worry her; she knows it is her version of nerves.

None of them has any idea what is happening to the cello soloist in her private dressing room. Suzy is about to play the Dvorak cello concerto. She adores the cello, she loves performing itself and has an increasingly impressive international career, but she can't manage the hours before the performance. She has just managed to stop herself from throwing up and is now pacing round the room, breathing deeply. She will have to be pushed to get her onto the stage – and then she will come in to her own and play like a dream!

If you ever suffer from nerves as a musician, rest assured: you are not alone! You may find that no one mentions their experience of nerves, but almost everyone has them to some degree.

The issue is not whether you have them or not, it is whether those nerves cripple you in any way.

In the story above, there are a variety of different experiences of nerves. Anita, Naomi and Lucy have nerves that they can manage. They know their own particular quirks and have ways of dealing with them. Chris, Dave and Suzy have far bigger problems to deal with and with all of them, these problems affect their quality of life. Dave has to use drugs to play at all, and Chris and Suzy manage to play well, but at an enormous cost to themselves.

- *How do your nerves stop you from giving a free, inspired performance and being the best performer you can be?*
- *Do they impinge on your enjoyment of music, your instrument and performing itself?*
- *Do they affect your quality of life in general?*

Adrenalin all around

We live in a society that runs on adrenalin. Everything is fast and everything has to have an element of drama in it to be considered exciting and worth bothering with. Ours is an instant society where there is never enough time. Everyone is busy, everyone rushes, and it is so easy to buy into it like everyone else, much as we might react against it. It is part of our emotional landscape and we barely even notice how much it is with us and around us.

A small dose of adrenalin can be an advantage when you are performing. It heightens everything, keeps you alert, ready to play at your best. But extreme nerves are debilitating and limit your ability to play well, as well as restricting your quality of life.

Masking the problem

Many musicians find their nerves unmanageable and try all sorts of ways to deal with them. Taking beta-blockers or similar adrenalin-reducing drugs is a very common choice and why not, when the drug can calm you to such an extent that your bow no longer shakes and your racing heartbeat lowers? It is so understandable. Many musicians drink alcohol before and after performances, to deal with nerves, the relief of stress, pressure and excess nervous energy.

The down side of any drugs is that there is the very real probability of becoming dependent on them. Even if there is no harm from being *physically* dependent, there is the issue of being *emotionally* dependent. Being dependent on drugs is disempowering. You are not in your full power as a person and a musician when you are dependent on a substance. You *need* it in order to function effectively.

Substances also numb you to your own feelings. Maybe that is what you want, because the reality without them is so unmanageable.

But if you are numb to your own feelings, how can you really play openly and expressively?

Do they really allow you to play from deep within, giving you profound fulfilment when you play, or are they just helping you survive the problem?

Are you thriving as a performer, or are you just surviving?

By finding ways of surviving an issue such as nerves, you are masking a problem that goes far deeper. If you decide to search out and understand what is at the bottom of your nerves, you have a far greater chance of both enjoying your performances and raising your quality of life.

- *What do you tend to do in order to control nerves before a performance?*

- *If you take substances to help calm you down, could these be hindering you from playing openly and expressively?*
- *Are you thriving as a performer, or are you just getting through each time?*

Crippling nerves

Extreme, crippling nerves come from *fear*. They stem from a primitive response to perceived danger. If you are out late at night in a dark alleyway, and you think someone is following you, you may very well be in danger. The adrenalin kicks in. All the blood rushes from your skin to your major organs, your heartbeat races, your muscles tense ready for action, your mental faculties sharpen, but from a place of fear and danger. You move into fight, flight or freeze.

In a performance situation, there is no actual physical danger. You are not being chased by a wild animal or frightened for your life in a dark alley. Instead, you are about to play music in front of an audience. This could be exhilarating, inspirational and fulfilling, but when the signals have got confused and everything is wild and out of balance, it is a case of surviving. You are reacting out of fear.

Think back to Chris, Dave and Suzy. Their nerves were extreme. Each was extremely fearful of making a mess of their performance, because that could have such repercussions for them in terms of their career. It was as if a primitive part of them felt they would die. Not physically, but emotionally.

It is genuinely terrifying to know that if your performance is sub-standard in any way you may not be offered future work.

Fear can come from a very deep place in us. Sometimes it is difficult to know why we are responding so violently when we feel we are rational and sensible human beings. After the fear of no work, the most obvious trigger for fear and the subsequent out-of-control nerves is the Inner Critic.

The Inner Critic on the rampage

Some years ago, I was asked to play three hymns for the funeral service of a very well known public figure. On paper it was one of the easiest jobs I had ever done, but it ended up being one of the most nerve-racking. I arrived at the church to discover that one of the hymns wasn't in the hymn book, so I had to get people to help me find another hymn book, which had to be brought in from another village.

I started beating myself up for not having double-checked the hymns beforehand, and for not being professional in my preparation.

I felt terrible at involving the grieving family with the issue of finding another hymnbook. I started imagining that the friends who had given me the job would also think I was unprofessional and never book me again, even though there was nothing I could have done about the situation in advance. I was beating myself up for getting so stressed out over playing a few simple hymns. Added to that, because the emotion in the church was palpable, I found myself feeling responsible for making sure that my part in the service was absolutely perfect to somehow make it all better for all the grieving relatives.

My Inner Critic was having a field day. It was all too much. I was putting myself under such immense pressure that I started shaking as soon as I played the first note.

In a performance situation, the Inner Critic can run riot. Just before you go on stage, you might judge yourself harshly for not having practised enough, not having prepared properly, terrified that your fallibility as a musician will show through.

You can put yourself under immense pressure, as Joanne did in a previous chapter. "It has got to be good – my career depends on it!" This is too much for anyone to deal with and totally unrealistic. You set yourself up for failure by thinking like this, and you certainly set yourself up for a good dose of nerves.

You beat yourself up thinking you are not going to perform well enough and you project that judgement onto the audience. "I can't play it – this is terrible" becomes "they will see I can't play it, they will see it is terrible and they will judge me for it." In reality, your audience is far less likely to judge you than you think they will.

Of course, you can't guarantee how someone else will respond. What you can do is take responsibility for whether or not you judge yourself.

Being your own saboteur

Being anxious and nervous about performing can either galvanise you to practise fantastically, or you may find you become your own saboteur. You may not be taking care of yourself, having enough breaks and giving yourself the best possibilities for playing well. You may unconsciously leave practising to the last minute so that you can blame the lack of time for not playing well rather than taking responsibility for being superbly prepared.

You can build up pictures in your mind that set you up for failure. You might imagine a scenario in which you mess up in front of your peers. You see an audition going badly and getting a rejection letter in the post. And because of your negative mindset, you may not even practise well enough, so that you then prove your point to yourself that you can't play.

The Inner Critic and its friend the Saboteur almost got the better of me at the funeral I mentioned earlier. Fortunately for everyone, I managed to come to my own rescue!

As I started to play the first hymn, I immediately realised how negatively I was talking to myself, blaming myself and sabotaging my ability to play beautifully and supportively for my friends and the grieving congregation. I could see what was happening and knew I had to do something. As I played, I started taking some long, deep breaths. I was surprised at how quickly I felt better. I kept repeating in my mind, "it's ok, it's ok", soothing myself and changing my thoughts from criticism to kindness. I could feel my jangled nerves calming very rapidly and by the end of the hymn, I was no longer shaking. This was the first time I had ever tried out a version of *Pause, Breathe, Kind Eyes* in a performance situation and I was bowled over by how effective it was. Afterwards, much to my amazement, I had nothing but thanks and positive comments. No one had any idea of the drama that had been going on inside my head!

The Instant Rescue Remedy

Times like these are a wonderful opportunity to remind yourself of the tools of transformation from the last chapter. Whenever you find yourself being critical or lurching into doom and despair, think of *Pause, Breathe, Kind Eyes*. Think about whether you are using *open or closed language.* If you are using negative, closed words such as "this won't work" or "I will never get this right", first of all notice what you are doing. Then see whether you can change them. "What can I do to make this work?" or "What if I *can* get this right?" will bring you to a more open, receptive place where you see possibilities rather than shut doors. And if you are finding it difficult to feel positive at all, use the *Emotional Guidance System* to go up to the next step, so that bit by bit you can climb up to a much more positive state.

- *If you have extreme nerves, are you aware of the fear that is underneath the nerves?*
- *How much is the Inner Critic a trigger for this fear?*
- *How have you managed to be kind to yourself when you have had extreme nerves?*
- *What would you do if you had that experience again?*
- *Who can you safely confide in, who will understand what you are experiencing?*

Know it well

Obvious as it may seem, you need to know the music that you are playing fantastically well before you walk on stage to play it. If you do anything less, there is a strong chance that you will have a good dose of nerves. Practising for a performance is like an iceberg. Only the tip shows in the water, but the rest of it is a vast mass underneath the water, hidden from view. An enormous amount of work has to go on for the performance to be successful.

Don't bury your head in the sand

Observe what you are doing in your practising and be careful not to kid yourself that you know a piece when you don't. Telling yourself "yes, I know that bit – it will be fine," if you don't really know it, won't help you when you are walking on stage with the mild panic that comes from not knowing something and fearing it will trip you up later. Or telling yourself "this is tricky – I won't do it now, I will do it later" can often mean that it is shelved for another day, and that other day may not come.

Walking onto the concert platform and seeing the passages that you have shelved and not dealt with come back to haunt you is not a pleasant experience, and can be disastrous for nerves.

Burying your head in the sand when practising is not an option; you end up paying for it in the end.

Prepare with kindness

Do your best to catch those negative thoughts that may bubble up, especially if you are practising for a performance. The Objective Observer technique will help to you rephrase these critical thoughts in your mind. Your practising needs to be done with kindness. Notice your Inner Critic whenever it pops up to the surface. Be kind to yourself for beating yourself up again, and be kind to yourself in whatever ways you feel you are not up to scratch. Use *Pause, Breathe, Kind eyes* whenever you need to. Stop and notice what is happening; breathe and give yourself space; and look at yourself with kindness. Notice that your entire nervous system starts to calm.

Building kindness into your preparation is one of the best things you can do to reduce your nerves.

If you were kinder to yourself when you made mistakes in your practising, you will feel infinitely more relaxed when you perform.

If you stop judging yourself when you practise, you will stop projecting outwards onto the audience. You won't feel they are judging you so much, and you will feel more relaxed and able to play.

- *How can you begin to build kindness into your practice routine?*
- *Think back to a recent practice time when you were hard on yourself. How could you rephrase what you thought so that it is kinder and more uplifting?*

Emotional preparation – going deeper

One of the downsides of being exposed to a lot of judgement as you are learning is that it encourages the suppression of feelings and emotions. If you feel that you might be judged at any moment, you don't feel safe enough to express your feelings. You would be too vulnerable to attack, real or imagined. But locking them up will only result in emotional constipation!

To play music, a musician needs feelings and emotions that flow. It is our inner emotional landscape that fuels our expression.

Shifting emotions from negative to positive

It is so easy to go onto a roll with negative thoughts. Have you ever talked yourself into feeling bad? Have you ever found yourself going on a negative rampage? It might go something like this:

"Oh God, I've got to go on stage right now...I feel terrible... I don't know that awful pizzicato passage... I know that's the one that will trip me up... And then they'll all think I can't play... And that'll mean I won't get that concert... And if I don't get that concert I can't show how well I can play... And if I can't do that... Well, I might as well forget it... Oh God, I've got to go on stage... H-e-e-l-l-p.... I'm going to mess this up, I just know it..."

This is such a powerful force of emotion and something that doesn't serve you at all. All those words and all those feelings are painting a picture of what can and probably will happen.

By energising these thoughts you are driving yourself towards a self-fulfilling prophecy.

But you have a choice. You can *choose* to change your inner talk and you start by bringing in the Objective Observer. The Objective Observer, with great empathy, observes what is going on.

"Wow – I am being really down on myself... I'm seeing everything really negatively... Is this really what I want? Is it helping me by feeling this? What do I want to feel? What would I like to see happen?"

Whilst still acknowledging the pressure and stress of the situation, you can place more positive thoughts alongside it as you step on to the stage. You might choose more encouraging thoughts that sound something like this:

"I'm about to go on stage... I do feel nervous... But... I really love playing so much... I love this piece... It would be so great if the audience really loved it too... They've all come to hear me play... I'd love to get through to

them... I'd love to move them with this amazing music... If I can inspire them that would feel really good... Yes, that does feel good... I'm actually looking forward to going on stage..."

Once you master the speed and passion of these positive emotional rampages, you will notice how quickly the Inner Critic just drops away and you find yourself in a wonderful space of feeling good. It is the perfect way to deal with nerves and an incredible way to prepare for performing. It opens you up and gets you in touch with your feelings. You can increase the effect of this by using techniques such as visualising.

How Sam used visualisation to give a stunning recital

Sam was a student of mine who had been worried about a particular recital, a whole year before she was due to perform it. She had been scared that it would go badly and that she wouldn't play well. Her playing had been full of the anxieties she was predicting she would feel about the concert.

I showed her, through some visualisation techniques, how she could choose to change her inner pictures from scared and anxious to positive and expectant.

She practised visualising every detail of her performance, seeing it exactly as she wanted it to be. She saw herself feeling good, being calm, being totally prepared, loving the experience of performing and she practised this as she practised the music, on a daily basis for a whole year.

In the recital hall, I watched her come onto the concert platform. She looked calm, confident and totally prepared. She settled herself, took time, breathed and started to play. She took complete, relaxed control of every aspect of her performance, managing the whole recital hall as well as managing herself. We were drawn in, mesmerised by her extraordinary playing and her incredible ability to communicate. I had to pinch myself to remember that this was the same student who had been so riddled with anxieties a whole year before.

Using your senses to imagine a fantastic performance

Hand in hand with the thoughts you think are the pictures you hold in your mind. Our imaginations are incredibly powerful. It is said that your unconscious mind doesn't know the difference between imagination and reality, which provides you with a phenomenal tool.

Instead of programming yourself for disaster and knowing you are going to have to deal with uncontrollable nerves, you can programme yourself for success.

If you check in to the way you normally see yourself perform and the feelings you have when you walk on stage, what are they? Are they positive and upbeat, excited about the performance, or are you actually setting yourself up for failure by imagining the performance not going well, and your nerves being out of control? Shining the light on that may well expose some important home truths.

Now imagine the performance in the way you would like it to be. You see yourself walk onto the concert platform, fantastically prepared, feeling wonderful. You feel all those good feelings in your body. You are really looking forward to playing. You hear the muffled silence of the audience expectant and eager to hear you perform.

You imagine those audience members absolutely on your side, keen to hear you perform well and loving the music you are playing.

Your senses are alive, you are ready. You make practical adjustments to prepare yourself and you imagine the music you are going to play, feeling the feelings of that music, really loving it. You hear the first note or notes in your head. And then you start...

How good would that feel? Good? Really good! And if that is not a normal experience for you, it can be from now on. But be aware, it may not be enough to just do this once. If you have some negative beliefs about performing and normally get very nervous, you may find that your negative mind-set outweighs the new, more positive mind-set.

So, start practising your performance with all the fantastic feelings that connect to it, as much as you practise the music.

If you find yourself back-sliding into negativity, don't start to beat yourself up; just gently turn your feelings and imagination back to the positive picture. If you continue to do this, you will find that before long you will be thinking and feeling totally differently about performing.

- *What opportunities do you have coming up to put these techniques into practice?*
- *How could you sustain the good feelings you are beginning to create?*

Physical preparation

From a physical perspective, you need to know what suits you best primarily in terms of *food* and *rest*. Everyone is different, and you do need to know what helps or upsets your particular system.

Being physically tired or tense is something that mustn't be ignored. Energy can't flow freely through a tired body. Assuming the concert is in the evening, you have a whole day ahead of you. If travelling is involved, you need to make sure that you have time to rest when you arrive. You may not be able to have the luxury of lying down in a quiet room, but you could, if you feel like it, lie down on the floor of the green room in the warm up pose that I talk about in Chapter 7: Finding physical freedom. Doing a few yoga poses or Tai Chi exercises can be very helpful. Tuning in to your body, as an athlete would, will help you to be physically prepared as possible.

Eating and drinking before a concert

People have very different views on when and what to eat before a performance. Most musicians I know eat after they perform, because they find that their digestion gets in the way of performing. My experience is totally different. I need to eat before I perform because otherwise I don't have the energy I need and I will often feel faint and disconnected. I learnt this the hard way, from experience.

I once gave a concert in Hong Kong in mid-summer and the air conditioning had just broken in the concert hall. The temperatures in Hong Kong in the summer are around 33C, with something in the region of 90% humidity. That in itself is not conducive to playing well, but coupled with the fact that I hadn't eaten, I was asking for trouble.

In the last page of the Brahms clarinet trio at the end of the concert, I nearly fainted. The music was swimming around in front of my eyes and I could barely make out any of the notes.

I found myself almost hanging onto the piano to stop myself from keeling over. I managed to make it to the end without any hiccups, but it was a red flag for me and I have always made sure I have eaten before a concert ever since.

If you do need to eat before a performance, but don't want a full meal, it is advisable to avoid anything that gives you a quick sugar rush. Anything that gives you an immediate high (chocolate bars, raisins, cakes, pastries) will bring you crashing down within quite a short space of time. This is not what you want in the middle of a performance. Instead, it is better to eat a slow release carbohydrate along with a small bit of protein. For example, an oat cake with a slice of cheese or a bit of peanut butter (without the extra sugar), or a piece of fruit with a few nuts. The protein helps to stabilise the sugar high so that it releases slowly into your bloodstream, giving you constant energy rather than an instant sugar rush. To explore this further, have a look into Patrick Holford's work on the Glycemic Load.

Caffeine and alcohol can be dangerous before concerts. Most musicians I know avoid caffeine like the plague because it can cause jitters, as well as give you too much of a high. All you need is a healthy amount of adrenalin.

Alcohol can make you drowsy or less focused. I do know people who swear by a small glass of wine to calm their nerves, and others who drink extensively to numb down more extreme nerves.

Getting rid of excess nervous energy

If a lion chases a gazelle in the animal world, the gazelle will immediately go into fight/flight response. If, for whatever reason, the lion doesn't catch her and she realises she is no longer in danger, her body goes into a process where it shakes off all the excess adrenalin. It is only then that she goes back to the herd, all the physical memories of the chase having gone from her body.

When musicians perform, there is both the build-up before the concert and also the coming down process afterwards. Many musicians say that they are often so 'wired' after a concert that it takes them a couple of hours to come back to normal again and readjust.

Excess physical energy before the concert can turn into overwhelming nerves, which can be very difficult to handle, as we have seen. After the concert, people tend to 'wind down' through alcohol or partying. What the body really needs is to shake it off physically.

Literally shaking the energy out can be fast and effective. Find somewhere appropriate and keeping both feet flat and firmly rooted to the ground, shake your body out as crazily as you feel like for a few minutes or as long as you need to.

I find that if I don't feel comfortable shaking, I need to do at least something physical to get rid of the excess nervous energy – going for a walk, cycling, or even dancing. It is extremely effective and saves me the two hours or so that it normally takes for the nervous energy to stop running round my system.

Make sure you have what you need

Try to make sure that you don't have too much else going on in your life that demands your urgent attention, and 'clear the space' for the concert.

What is really important is that you do whatever you need to do in order to be in the best frame of mind for the concert.

The organisers of the concert are not necessarily performers and may not understand your particular needs, so it is important that you make sure that you ask for what you need. Give yourself time and space in the green room. You don't have to chat to the organisers. You can politely extract yourself and stay quiet if that is what you need.

People deal with this time differently. Some would prefer to chat, as long as it is trivia and nothing to do with the concert. It keeps their mind off what they are about to play and stops them needlessly worrying about what they are about to do. Others need silence and no interruptions. You may like to be alone if you are using any of the techniques we have looked at to help you deal with nerves.

The bubble

The bubble is something that I would recommend to any musician to use, particularly as they are preparing for a concert. The bubble is an imaginary means of protection that has enormous energetic power. Imagine surrounding yourself in a bubble. The bubble can be made of anything you would like it to be – the soap bubbles children blow, translucent bubble gum – whatever takes your fancy. It can be as colourful as you like both inside and out, and it is invisible. It can also change in size and shape. If you are playing in a concert, it could envelop both you and your instrument in a comforting personal space, or it can shrink to body size if you are physically very close to people in the next desk in an orchestra.

Inside your bubble you are completely safe. Anything that does not serve your highest interests can bounce off and go elsewhere. The Inner Critic has no place here and it is here that the Inner Critic can transform.

Creating the bubble is only half the story. The second half is what goes inside it. Inside the bubble are good feelings. You need to fill your bubble with the best feelings you can find. You are looking for simple things: a lovely memory of building a snowman as a child, the stunning sunset you have just seen, blossom on a tree, mist on the hills, a hug from your boyfriend or girlfriend. It doesn't matter what it is; what is important is that it makes you feel good.

This is extremely powerful. You are creating a field of endorphins around you. If you were to look more closely into what happens when you create a field of endorphins around you, you would find that your body chemistry shifts. Real physical, chemical changes take place inside that have a monumental impact on your world.

- *Are you aware of any food or drink intolerances that might upset your system and be best avoided 24 hours before a performance?*
- *Are you someone who needs to withdraw into a quiet space or distract yourself by socialising before a performance?*
- *If you were to create a comforting bubble around you, what might you put in it?*

Loving the music supports your nerves

The love you have for music is there to sustain you through all the challenges that come your way. Without that love, you might as well not be doing it. It is the joy that you have for playing incredible, beautiful music, the love you have for your instrument, that helps you overcome any obstacles. One of those obstacles is nerves.

Loving the music is one of the best ways for dealing with uncontrollable nerves. Putting your focus on the music, and what you love about it, enables you to put everything into perspective.

You climb back into the big picture again and your panic about what someone in the audience might think about your playing falls away unnoticed. The Inner Critic is nudged off its perch, down into an area of far lesser importance, and you move into a much higher feeling place. You have shifted up the ladder on the Emotional Guidance System, nearer to the positive feelings at the top and further from the negative feelings at the bottom. People talk about getting into the zone or the flow when they play, and *being passionate about the music* is one way.

But what if you regularly have to play music you don't like, or that doesn't inspire you?

Someone else's choice

I spent many years playing music that was always someone else's choice. There was always music that inspired me and lifted me, and then there was music that I was just playing because I had to and I was being paid for it. I found myself getting numb and feeling as if I was a cog in a wheel, doing what I felt I had to, rather than being inspired by playing a composer's extraordinary music. Once I realised what was happening, I started making sure I was always learning music that *I* had chosen, whether or not I was performing it or being paid for doing it. I just needed that reminder to get in touch with what I loved about the music.

Your relationship with music is like any relationship. You need to keep the love alive; you don't want to take the relationship for granted or use it only as a means of earning a living.

Nor do you want the relationship to grow stale. Keep it fresh, stay in love with it, because this is what it is all about. It makes all the difference when it comes to performance. Love for the music is what is at the heart of it all.

- *Can you think of times when you have had to play music you just couldn't love?*
- *Why was that?*
- *How could you keep your love of music alive if it is threatened?*

Summary

We've now built up a number of strategies which will help you to gain control of nerves and the Inner Critic, and begin to clear out the unwanted "stuff" inside, so that you can truly play with passion "from the inside out".

- **The first step** is to know your nerves. How crippling are they, and how much they are stopping you from playing from your heart?

- **The second step** is to look at how you can prepare yourself for important performances in terms of bringing kindness and positive thinking into your practice routines.

- **The third step** is how you can take care of your emotional and physical requirements on the day and just before your performance.

- **The fourth step** is how you can take the heat out of crippling nerves just as you step out onto the stage, by choosing and using whichever of the emergency rescue remedies you find most effective.

In Chapter 6 we will look at what happens when the body itself has had enough, throwing strain and pain at you, driving you to doctors and sometimes to despair.

6

What causes the pain?

> *Your pain is the breaking of the shell that encloses your understanding.*
> **Khalil Gibran**

Sarah's arms were giving her pain, and they had done for over ten years. She had been passed from pillar to post in the medical community, with no-one agreeing exactly what the problem was. Some said it was carpal tunnel syndrome, others that it was tendonitis, and others still said that there was something wrong with the way her nerves were positioned in her right arm. She had had ultra sound, MRI scans, a cortisone injection and even an operation to change the position of a nerve in her arm, but nothing had made any difference.

The pain she had suffered and the mixed medical opinions had stopped her from pursuing a music degree specialising in performance, and she was now desperate.

She felt that she couldn't get on with any alternative career until she had sorted out what was happening to her arms.

Sarah was extremely intuitive. She knew that what was happening to her was much more than a series of physical symptoms, and that there were strong emotional triggers. She admitted being a very anxious performer, and it was for this reason that a rheumatologist from BAPAM (British Association for Performing Arts Medicine) had passed her on to me.

I discovered that Sarah's problems arose from when she was a very young child. Her parents had divorced when she was six and her relationship with her them was difficult. As an only child, she was shared between them, each of them fighting for her love with more and more gifts and treats. She started learning the piano at the time of her parents' divorce and became good very quickly with the support of a wonderful teacher.

The piano became her refuge and she poured all her anguish and mixed up emotions into music.

So many musicians bump up against physical pitfalls at one stage or another throughout their education and career. These problems can cause immense distress and can put a halt to learning and performing for a period of time, or even for good. They are always complex. Problems such as tendonitis or nodules for singers are not just what they appear on the outside. Scratch the surface and all sorts of emotional and psychological issues start to appear, wanting to tell their story.

Accepting the body-mind connection is essential here. If these problems are dealt with simply as physical symptoms, as with Sarah, the musician is unlikely to improve.

They have to be looked at from many different angles and with an open approach. It has to be truly holistic and the issues need to be seen as part of the person's entire life.

The big taboo

At the first signs of a physical problem that seriously affects their playing or singing, most musicians will go into panic mode. A student may tell their teacher but will be very hesitant about telling anyone else. They don't want to be seen to have anything wrong at all.

Having something wrong brings up the biggest of all fears, which is: "I will never be able to play or sing again and my career will be over."

The professional can't tell anyone, even his close colleagues, for fear of not getting any work. For the student it is similar. It may not be an issue of not getting work, but the fears are still immense. "What if I can't do that audition/competition/recital? I can't miss out on all those opportunities."

It is a terrible secret to bear on your own.

It is terrible if you can't share it with someone who understands, who doesn't judge you and who doesn't think your career is automatically over.

The strong tendency is to continue to hide the problem and to feel ashamed of it. Shame can be very strong and the best possible way to deal with it is to share it with someone. You need to pick someone who you know will listen and not judge you. The very act of sharing it can be such a relief that you find yourself part way towards healing the problem.

And then there is denial. If you don't feel you can talk to anyone, and the thought of dealing with the issue face on is too stressful, you push it down and deny that it is there.

You pretend everything is as normal. But deep down you are sick with worry and desperate for it to all go away.

You might feel that having physical symptoms implies that you are not doing something well enough. You might even feel that you are not a good enough musician, because how could something like this have happened otherwise? All these concerns pile up on top of the issue itself and perpetuate it.

Denying that there is something wrong can be dangerous. It can only get worse if you don't deal with it. What you need at this point is to see it all from a bigger perspective. All that is happening is that you have just got things a little out of balance.

You are not broken and you don't need fixing.

With encouragement, support and understanding, you can get to the root of the issue, tackle the physical symptoms and move back into wellness. It is all possible!

Pain as an indicator

Pain and even discomfort is a warning indicator. It is a red flag, alerting you that something needs to be addressed. The last thing you want to do at this point is to push on through the pain, aggravating the physical symptoms further and causing no end of possible damage.

"No pain, no gain" has been a motto in the past and it has no place in this context. Pain is a wake-up call alerting you to take action.

Think about it this way. If a red light appears somewhere on the dashboard of a car, it is showing that something is not working quite right. It may be something straightforward or it may be more serious. You would take it to a garage to get it checked out because in the most serious case, you know you could put your life in danger. But would you instead take the bulb out of the irritating red light so that you could ignore it? Would you think that if the red light is not there then the problem has gone away? I would be surprised if you did. And yet that is what so many people do to their bodies when they come up against physical playing problems.

- Are you aware of any specific physical problem when you play?
- How do you feel about it?
- Are you worried about the consequences of telling someone about it?
- Has your symptom got worse over a period of time?
- Are there any circumstances under which it gets better?

The body-mind connection

Susanna was a talented pianist who had had debilitating tendonitis for six years by the time I first saw her. During the first session we had together, I asked her when she first had signs of the condition and what else was happening in her life at the same time.

83

***She told me that her grandmother had died during those few months.
Her grandmother had been her first piano teacher and her best friend.
Saying this, she burst into tears.***

*She was just starting to realise how related the two issues were. The more
she looked at it, the more she realised that she was also feeling guilty that
she couldn't play well anymore and that she felt she was letting her
grandmother down. It was so clear that there was a strong emotional
charge whenever she played the piano and that this had manifested itself
physically in the form of tendonitis.*

*Once she had begun to recognise what was going on deep down, she
was then able to start the process of learning what she was doing physically
and how to move on from that.*

Emotions can get locked into the body and stay there until they are
addressed. Susanna made extraordinary progress from that day onwards
because it was as if she had let the cork out of the bottle. The emotional
charge had gone and she 'only' had to deal with the physical side after
that.

***Physical issues without the emotional reasons fuelling them are much
simpler to manage. But trying to deal with physical symptoms without
addressing the emotional side rarely works.***

*Maria had a similar experience of deep emotions seizing her up physically.
She was sixteen and about to start her A-level course when she came to me
with shooting pains in her wrists and arms, distraught because she could
barely play. I suspected there was something more going on.*

Very quickly, it became apparent that she was having a battle with her

84

parents. Her father, a forceful man, did not wholeheartedly support Maria's passion for the piano, and grudgingly paid for lessons. She had to work to find the money to go on music courses because he wouldn't pay. He wanted her to do science A-levels with the aim of reading medicine at University, and even though she was good at the sciences, she definitely didn't want to do medicine. All she wanted to do was to play the piano. She felt passionately about it, and this not seeing eye to eye had led to shouting matches between her and her father.

In just one session, she realised that she wasn't in a position to change her father's outlook, but that she could change her own response to it.

I encouraged her to make her own choice within the rather difficult situation she found herself in.

She decided it was easier to accept what her father wanted and go ahead with the science A-levels, knowing that by the time she was eighteen, she would be in a much stronger position to make her own choices about whether or not she would study medicine, and ultimately how she would lead her life.

What was important for her was to know that she was not powerless in the face of her father. She was aware that fighting him at this stage was counter-productive. From the outside, it appeared that not much had changed. Inwardly, everything had changed. She realised that by making her own decision, she felt completely empowered. I could see that she understood what it meant to take her own power back. A girl who had been in a state of collapse and distress an hour before was now standing tall and smiling.

By the end of that day, she had stopped taking all her painkillers and within a week her pain had gone.

The emotional issue at the core had been addressed, so from then on, I focused on re-educating her into healthier playing habits. I talked to her six months later and her pain had never returned. But more important than any of that, she was more in alignment with herself and much happier.

It is wonderful when it works like this. You hit on the right underlying cause, and the physical symptoms resolve themselves over time with some support. In Maria's case it was also essential to make the time to talk rather than automatically go to the instrument for the answer.

That initial hour of talking saved her months of pain.

It meant that she could then focus on what she was doing physically and change what was not working so that she could play well.

One of the reasons Maria was able to make such a speedy recovery was because she was dealing with a recent issue that hadn't had a chance to settle and take hold in her body.

- *If you are experiencing pain or tension, do you have a sense of what else was happening in your life when the problem started?*
- *Could you see the value of talking about emotional issues in your background if there seemed to be a connection to your pain?*

Beliefs and their impact on the body

How you think and what you believe also has an impact on the body. If you think the same thing enough times, it becomes a belief. Negative beliefs lodge themselves into the body over time. It is as if they root themselves like a weed that is hard to dig up.

Common beliefs are things like perfectionism – the belief that something has no value if it is not perfect, and a symptom of perfectionism is 'trying too hard'. 'Trying too hard' is connected with the belief that it is a bad thing to make a mistake. (We looked at this in Chapter 3: The Bully and Chapter 4: The Inner Critic.)

When you impose perfectionism on yourself and you try too hard, the flow is disrupted and tightness occurs in the body. This, unchecked, can turn into some form of physical problem.

Chloe had repeated difficulties in keeping freedom and flexibility because of her need to play everything perfectly. On one occasion she found that she couldn't manage a passage that, given her technical capability, should have been extremely easy. We looked at the problem from a number of different angles, but it seemed that the more we tackled it, the worse it got.

She was playing the passage very unevenly and with no rhythm at all. She was puzzled and quite distressed that she was playing so 'badly', and feeling that her body was not cooperating. Her body was in fact cooperating very efficiently given what she was feeding it.

The issue was not simply physical. Chloe couldn't bear mistakes. She couldn't bear making them and she couldn't bear hearing them. The fear of making a mistake was so powerful in her that her muscles would clench in anticipation. She then couldn't play even the simplest passage. Chloe didn't have tendonitis, but the tension she was building up in her arms from her need to be perfect was so strong that she was heading in the direction of tendonitis.

Trying too hard

Musicians are very prone to trying too hard, and this happens because there is this fear of making mistakes. Nobody wants to make mistakes, so you have to try hard *not* to make those mistakes. And along with this, the challenges of mastering the skills of your instrument and playing to a professional level are immense. So, trying hard is necessary. Or is it? I believe that it is not trying hard or putting in effort that is required; it is energy, focus and a good dose of commitment that you need. And the energy and focus need to come from a place of ease and freedom. I will be expanding on this in the next chapter.

'Trying too hard' results in physical tensions to a greater or lesser degree. I have seen so many students over the years show almost imperceptible flickers of tension in their bodies from their over-eager desire to play well.

Sometimes they would appear to be completely free in their playing, but I could intuitively sense the tension. And when I picked up their arm, I could actually feel it. The minuscule tightenings are the start of more seriously engrained troubles, and if they're not addressed, their effect is compounded.

- *Are you aware of trying so hard to play well that you can actually sense the slow build-up of tension?*
- *Can you sense or feel where this is happening in your body?*

But I never think about my body!

Physical problems come about for all sorts of reasons, but always, somewhere in the mix, is a lack of body awareness. You need to understand your body and how it relates to your technique and your playing. A technique can have been acquired over the years with no real understanding of how the body works, what puts strain on different joints and tendons, and what the body can deal with. At a fundamental level, your playing needs to be physically free so that you don't tighten up and give yourself problems. It needs to be efficient so that you don't put any unnecessary extra strain and tension on your body, and it needs to be free in order that you can express yourself freely.

Even if you have been fabulously taught, and have a stunning technique, you can still ignore your body on a regular basis.

You as a musician need to be as aware of your body as an athlete is. After all, playing music is a physical activity and is in many ways athletic. An athlete will be conscious of the food he eats, what he drinks, the amount of rest he takes before a race or a match, how much he warms up. He needs to be sensitive to every fine detail of how his body is functioning, and if an athlete is injured in a high profile situation, there is a physiotherapist at hand immediately to give the best care.

Overuse and misuse

One of the most commonly held views musicians have about getting physical playing-related problems is that they come from too much practice. In one sense they are right, but not entirely. You should be able to practise for a number of hours a day (depending on your instrument and what it allows) without any physical concerns, but only if you are treating your body well and looking after it. The problems come when you are practising for long hours and doing something that is not good for your body. It is the combination of overuse and misuse that is the issue. You can get away with misuse if you don't practise much, and you can get away with overuse if you aren't mistreating your body. But you can't get away with both.

- *Are you taking your body for granted, expecting it just to do its job?*
- *Are you conscious of taking care of your body as an athlete would?*

"Oh no, it's my bag!"

Rachel was a flautist who had pains in her right arm that were causing her problems when she played. She had never had much thought about how she was using her body until the problem arose, and then the incentive for playing well again was so strong, that she started exploring what she was doing. When she came to me, I could see that she was tensing up her right upper arm in a way that was more than was necessary for holding the flute. I noticed at the same time that she had come in with a very large bag that she had slung over her right shoulder. She told me that someone had given her the bag for her birthday and she had only been using it for a couple of months.

"I love this bag," she told me. "For the first time I can fling everything into it, including my flute... It means I don't forget anything anymore!"

"Except," I added, "that you have forgotten how to hold the flute well with your right arm. You have started to hold your flute as if it were a heavy bag!" She looked at me and then it dawned on her.

The pain in her right arm had started around her birthday, when she had first used the bag.

So we looked at different ways that she could hold her bag that would stop her putting strain on to her right arm. I also pointed out to her that it looked as if there had been a mild problem of tensing her right arm anyway, but that it had been exacerbated by the way she was holding the bag. With this information, and with a way of holding her bag that was less stressful, she was able to go away and observe what she was doing with the flute.

A week later, she was back with lots more insights. The pains had lessened considerably and she put a lot of that down to the much better way she was now holding her bag. But she had also noticed, with her heightened sense of body awareness, that she was, as I had thought, very subtly lifting her right arm from the shoulder when she played. She had a strong sense that this had been something she had done for years, but that it had never been an issue until the episode with the bag had highlighted it.

I showed her ways of freeing her arms from her shoulders by shaking them out at her side. With a free upper body and free arms, she was then able to lift up the flute without the very slight, tense holding she had been doing.

After a number of weeks, she rang me to say that the pains had gone and she was able to play the flute without holding her arm in the way that had contributed to the problems.

Rachel shows that it is not always just the instrument that causes physical problems. It can also be something that seems completely unconnected. If you have problems playing your instrument, check to see whether there is anything that you have been doing recently that is different and that might have exacerbated any low-lying problem that is already there.

The two keyboards: the piano and the computer

In trying to resolve problems with your instrument, you may realise that some other activity is jeopardising your progress. This is exactly what happened to Oliver.

Oliver was studying to become a professional pianist. He had pains in his hands and arms which wouldn't shift. For two years, I worked with him to show him how to free up his hands and wrists. We worked in immense detail, covering every aspect of his technique, but the pain was still there. I found this puzzling because he understood everything I was showing him, and he was putting it into action immediately in the lesson. We repeated the same exercises over and over again with no improvement.

I then realised that I needed to look at the bigger picture. I asked him how else he spent his time apart from practising, and he told me about his passion for writing. I was amazed because I had had no idea how much he loved to write! He told me that he wrote every day at the computer and sometimes for quite a few hours a day.

I had some suspicions of what might be at the bottom of his inability to make progress at the piano, and asked him to go to my computer and show me how he typed.

And there it was! He was hunched over the computer, sitting at the wrong height and virtually stabbing the keys. What was intriguing was that he had not made a connection between the piano and the computer. He hadn't registered that they were both keyboards and that one was affecting the other.

I showed him how to use the computer so that he didn't halt his progress at the piano and he began to realise that he could improve his piano playing all he liked, but if he didn't change the way he sat at the computer, he wasn't going to shift his tendonitis.

How to sit at the computer

Sitting at the computer is something that everyone now does on a daily basis. It is common to see people, musicians or otherwise, in the most unnatural positions at their lap tops, slouching, stretching out their arms, having the computer at the wrong height and so on. There are equally an unprecedented number of people in the workforce at large who are suffering with Repetitive Strain Injury from the way they are using computers. Because of this, I think it is important to address the basic principles of how to sit at a computer in order that you don't give yourself unnecessary problems that could easily affect the way you play your instrument.

- Take a chair that is comfortable and simple, ideally something that has a hard back and a straight seat and that can be softened with a cushion.
- Now sit on the front half of the chair with your feet flat on the floor, your arms out in front of you, resting from the elbow up to your hands. You are sitting on the front half of the chair so that you support yourself from your abdominal muscles rather than your thighs, which you do if you sit further back.
- Then you need to make sure that your elbows are level with the table or desk so that you really can rest your lower arms on the surface.

93

- Your upper arms need to be relaxed and free, as do your lower arms. Aim to have your lower arms as relaxed as possible and only use the minimum amount of effort of your hands and fingers for the keyboard and mouse.
- Be aware too that your hands shouldn't grip, particularly when holding the mouse.

The computer is probably the most important 'other' activity to be aware of. But there are plenty more culprits.

Here are some of the main ones you may not have thought of:

Driving

If you drive, and you drive on a regular basis, stop to think next time you take the steering wheel.

- Are you gripping the steering wheel?
- Are your shoulders up round your ears?
- Are you generally tense?

Think about letting go of your shoulders and loosening your grip. A tight grip on the steering wheel can translate straight across to playing your instrument.

When you are stationary at traffic lights, give yourself a few seconds to check in and see how you are doing. Remember to breathe deeply! Breathing helps you free up and calm, which is a wonderful antidote to feeling stressed as you drive.

It is advisable to sit reasonably close to the steering wheel so that your legs are flexed and not stretched straight out, because it allows the lower back to be freer. You may also need a small cushion in the small of your back for support.

Mobile phones

The next time you pick up your mobile, notice what you are doing to your arms, hands and shoulders.

- Are you gripping it tightly?
- Do you clench your hands when you write a text?
- Are you one of the people who hold a phone under your ear whilst you are doing other things?

Doing this means that you are scrunching up your shoulder and neck and possibly exacerbating whatever problems you may already have playing your instrument.

Handwriting

Handwriting is not the issue that it used to be because people write with pens far less than before. But if you do need to write with a pen, especially in the pressurised atmosphere of exams, beware!

A clenched hand when writing can cause all sorts of problems. Your handwriting style was learnt when you were at primary school and it probably hasn't changed much since. Whether or not you gripped your pencil at the age of five will have its impact much later on, because nobody really thinks about changing how they hold their pen as an adult. Check that your arm is free and that you are just using your hand, freely, to write without involving the whole arm.

Even brushing your teeth!

Watch to see if you are cleaning your teeth by moving your whole arm in a clenched position. Again, like holding a pen, make sure your arm is free and that you are just using your hand when you are moving your toothbrush.

- *If you have had a sudden flare-up of pain, could you relate it to something different you have been doing, like carrying a new bag or helping a friend lift heavy boxes?*
- *Are you aware of anything that you are doing in your everyday life that could cause pain and negatively impact the playing of your instrument?*

So what can I do to be free of pain?

You have various different options you can choose from. There is the conventional medical route or the holistic route, which explores a number of bodywork techniques and alternative therapies. It is really a case of following what intuitively feels right for you.

Ultimately, you may well need to find an approach that will enable you to get to the bottom of what is causing the problem as well as heal the symptoms.

Most importantly, you want to be able to go back to your instrument and build in new, positive habits that will enable you to play well, and this needs to be permanent.

So let's say you have developed what is loosely called 'tendonitis'. Tendonitis is a very broad tem for inflamed tendons. The GPs themselves would be the first to admit that it is an umbrella term for physical problems that don't fall neatly into any specific category. I am similarly using it as a catch-all term, to keep it simple.

The medical route

If you choose to go down the conventional medical route, your first step would be to go to your GP, who may or may not be familiar with this kind of problem. You are likely to be told that you need to rest it for a period of time so that the tendons can reduce their inflammation and you can start getting better. This is sensible advice, but it is only dealing with the physical symptoms.

You may be sent to any number of specialists who will most likely advise rest, cortisone injections or even operations. Out of these, the safest and least intrusive is to rest. Cortisone injections may lessen the pain and sort the problem out over the short term, but they are rarely a long term solution. Operations are really a last resort. However brilliantly skilled the surgeon, it is a big risk to take.

From my experience of seeing musicians who have had operations, they almost always regret having them because their symptoms at best stay the same or at worst, go downhill.

I can't remember being aware of a musician who has really benefited from an operation, particularly one that is supposed to sort out their playing problems. An operation that goes wrong can put your career and well-being at risk.

Bodywork techniques

Over the last thirty years or so, musicians have become increasingly aware of different types of bodywork and alternative therapies that can be very supportive to their playing.

The Alexander Technique has been phenomenally important in helping body awareness in musicians, and many a career has been saved by working with talented and experienced Alexander teachers. Other disciplines that have been welcomed by musicians are Feldenkrais, Tai Chi, yoga and Pilates.

On *Chamber Music International*, a chamber music course I founded and directed from 2000-2007, two hours every afternoon was dedicated either to Feldenkrais, Tai Chi or Yoga. Many of those students, who are now professional players, use one of those disciplines to warm up and free up before performances. They swear by them!

There is now a charity which specialises in helping musicians and dancers deal with any problems they might come across. BAPAM has gathered together an impressive list of medical practitioners, from GPs through to rheumatologists, alongside counsellors, osteopaths, chiropractors, Alexander Technique teachers – the list is endless. It is a very good first step to take if you have no idea which way to turn.

BAPAM is a charity specifically set up for performing- related problems. You know that they will take you seriously and that they have a lot of very good practitioners to choose from.

A holistic approach and re-education

It can be devastating when pain is preventing you from playing, and you will do anything to get back to your instrument again. A cortisone injection will not sort out what caused the problems in the first place, and neither will an operation. Even the best treatment from the best practitioners in the alternative therapy world may just help relieve the symptoms. Rest and no intervention at all may get you just as far or possibly further. If you then go back to your instrument doing the same things that caused the problem in the first place, you are not going to heal.

What will work for you on a much more profound level is a holistic approach. It is difficult to do this on your own. Ideally you need someone who can help unravel the underlying causes, who understands the impact this is having on you and who can help you re-educate your thoughts, your feelings and your body. Alternatively, you may find it useful to work with the questions in this chapter to help you towards a different way of thinking.

You may well have performances lined up, and the psychological effect of cancelling performances is immense.

You will need support and guidance, particularly from someone who understands your world.

Usually for a musician, it is not the severity of the pain that is the issue. It is what that pain represents in terms of your future playing ability.

- *What have you tried so far to alleviate your symptoms, and are you happy that it has really dealt with the cause?*

99

- *Have you wondered whether a holistic technique, such as bodywork or emotional counselling, would help?*

Change and the pay-off for staying stuck

Change can be threatening to you and your way of life. It is easy to say that you want change. Of course you want your playing problem to clear up as soon as possible, but when it comes to facing what might be the root cause, you will probably find that a part of you wants to change and a part of you doesn't.

What is at stake when you change?

There might be a big pay-off for staying unwell, and your injury can be masking something you don't want to look at.

Are the nodules that you have just discovered on your vocal cords telling you that you find singing incredibly stressful, and that you would unconsciously go to any extreme just to stop experiencing this level of stress? Making a conscious decision to stop singing because you find it stressful could be much more demanding than unconsciously letting your emotions manifest as symptoms that do the job for you. It also means you can 'blame' the symptoms. "I can't sing because I have nodules" can be so much easier than "I need to deal with *why* I find singing so stressful". You need to be prepared to face what is going on underneath the symptoms and explore what your body is trying to communicate. It also means taking responsibility for your own emotional and physical health and wellbeing.

Invested in being ill

Maddie came to me specifically to work with her tendonitis. She was a keen and talented violinist who had moved to the UK from Australia a few months before to finish her medical studies with her husband, who was a doctor. I worked with her for a few weeks, helping her to see how she was tensing up when she played, and giving her all sorts of exercises to improve her body awareness. She did incredibly well and it seemed as if she was going to move through the tendonitis in a matter of weeks. She talked animatedly about how happy she was when she left the sessions we had together, because she could see herself getting so much better.

And then everything suddenly changed. She stopped progressing as fast and decided to come for sessions less often. I was totally puzzled. I couldn't work out what was going on, until she started telling me a bit about her life in general. She had Chronic Fatigue Syndrome as well as tendonitis, and she had been ill with it for over five years. She had had vague, indefinable illnesses as a child and had always been seen as the sickly one and the invalid in the family. Her husband had met her when she was ill.

The more we talked, the more I started to understand that she was invested in being ill.

Not only that, but that she was used to being seen as ill. Her family saw her as ill and now her husband saw her as ill. Her role in her marriage was as the invalid. If she changed that now, she risked changing the entire basis on which her marriage had been founded. She was new to England and hadn't yet built her own life here. Much as a part of her clearly wanted to get well, there was too much at stake. She needed to survive, and she couldn't risk jeopardising her marriage in a new country. In the end she stopped coming to the sessions, and I didn't hear from her after that.

What change can look like

Joe was an extremely talented jazz pianist who had seized up with pains in both arms and had no idea what to do about it. His approach to piano technique was to do whatever it took to play the notes, and he had copied the style of a number of jazz pianists. His shoulders were rounded and he flung his hands at the keys with stiff arms. His body was simply not working as it needed to in order to play well and keep him fit and healthy. It was affecting his work and he was worried.

Joe needed to relearn everything and to understand what piano technique was all about. We started from square one. I asked him to stop all playing, all rehearsals, all his gigs and any commitments related to playing so that he could give his entire attention to relearning his physical approach to the piano.

Joe was on a three-month journey that was like learning to walk again.

I started by showing him how to sit well and then how to play one note with a free arm and with power rather than force. Then we built up to two notes and then five fingers, followed by five fingers in both hands. The next stage for him was to play a riff to see whether he could manage that with a free arm and power rather than force. After this, he started to manage a few minutes of improvisation. It took patience and dedication, but Joe's incentive was strong and he persevered even at the points that he was aching to play again.

Once he had mastered the ability to play well in the privacy of his own practice room, it was time to learn to keep the same way of healthy way of playing when rehearsing with his trio. We agreed that I would sit next to him whilst he rehearsed and click my fingers if he tightened up. This was so that he could stay aware whilst the rest of him was concentrating on the music and how he was communicating with the other players. Towards the end of the three months, he was ready to perform in front of an audience and I went to see him perform in a prestigious venue in central London.

He was a changed player: the round shoulders had disappeared, he was no longer flinging his hands at the keys.

He was now sitting upright at the keys, with a free back and arms, and he was playing with colours and sounds I had never witnessed from him before.

His pain had completely gone, and he told me that he wouldn't be playing the piano professionally if he hadn't had that time of starting from scratch.

There is always a gift that comes with situations that can, at the time, seem so bleak.

It is as if sometimes our bodies have to shout loudly at us to listen to what is really important.

So many people who have dealt with these type of problems have come out of them with powerful insights. They are often changed people. Joe's gift was immense. He learnt how to use his body well at the piano, what good piano technique was all about and to build it up himself. He learnt the importance of body awareness, how to be patient and what commitment and dedication can do when you have something you need to achieve.

Summary

If you are struggling with pain or other symptoms that are interfering with your playing or singing, here are some steps you can take.

- **The first step** is to acknowledge that if your symptom won't go away, you may need to think more broadly about what has caused it.

- **The second step** is to see if you can pinpoint anything that was happening in your life, whether it was an emotional trauma long ago, or a physical accident, or something more recent.

- **The third step** is to decide whether emotional counselling or one of the physical bodywork techniques would bring you most comfort and relief.

- **The fourth step** is to find the right person to help you.

Getting to the root of what our pain is trying to tell us enables us to banish the pain and enjoy our own gifts as musicians.

In the next chapter we will see how to free up the flow of energy through the body, so you can perform with effortless power.

7

Finding physical freedom

Take your finger and put it on your arm. Leave it there for about a minute and then take it off again. What you will find is that the action of putting your finger on your arm is noticeable. You can feel it. Then as you leave it there, you find that you lose awareness of your finger on your arm. Nothing has changed; it is still there, but you are not aware any longer. Then you take your finger off, and you notice something happening again, a difference in sensation.

This is how easy it is to lose awareness of our body, and equally, how easy it is to find it again.

It is vital to have an awareness of your body as a musician if you are to play your instrument well and effectively. Without it, you don't notice the build-up towards possible physical problems that we looked at in the last chapter. Twinges occur every now and again to attract our attention. Listening to them gives us a fantastic barometer for how we are doing and gives us an opportunity to act, before they become full-blown pain.

Tuning in to tension

Before I start practising, I like to use the following body awareness exercise as a warm up. I find that it is fantastic for getting me in touch with tension in my body. The key to this is to 'tune in' to your body, see where you are holding tension and then let go as much as you are able. It is a very similar position to that advocated by Alexander of the Alexander Technique, in which you lie on the floor with your knees up and your feet flat on the floor. This is my version:

- Lie on the floor with your head on a slim book and your back flat on the floor.
- Using a simple, straight chair (as opposed to an office chair or an armchair), lie so that your lower legs are resting across the seat.
- You need to make sure your knees are at a right angle and that the chair comfortably meets the backs of your knees. If not, put a cushion on the seat of the chair so it is at the right height.

I prefer this slight variation to the Alexander Technique position because by putting your legs over a chair, you take the pressure off the lower back and your legs can 'let go' completely.

Now tune in to your whole body.

- Is your neck free and relaxed?
- Are your shoulders carrying tension, and can you let them go?
- How is your breathing? Can you allow your lungs to expand fully?

- How are your abdominal muscles: are they holding tight?
- Are you tensing your buttocks, legs and feet?
- Once you start noticing the different areas in which you are holding tension, see whether you can release them.
- Breathe deeply and imagine the breath going to all the tense spots in your body and freeing them up. Keep breathing and allow your mind to float, whilst your main focus is on your body.
- Wait until you feel as if you have let go of as much tension as you can and that you feel free and at ease. You may find that you want to stay in this position for a few minutes or maybe anything up to half an hour.
- When you are ready, very gently roll onto one side and come up to sitting, then standing.

You will find that as you do this, ideally on a daily basis, you will start noticing more and more where your body has been taking the strain from what you have been doing habitually. This is the first step towards an awareness that is essential for playing.

It may be hard to believe, but this simple exercise can also be extraordinarily effective in an immediate relief of a lot of aches and pains. A sixteen-year-old came to me recently complaining of backache that was causing her considerable pain. She did this exercise for less than five minutes and told me that she felt much better afterwards, with hardly any back pain.

The sum of its parts

No matter whether you are a singer, a cellist or a flautist, performing music involves your *whole* body and not just the separate parts. It is easy to separate yourself into compartments. String players play with their hands and arms but may not think about their legs; pianists play with their hands and arms but may not be aware of their breath; woodwind players and brass players play with their facial muscles and breath but may not think about their shoulders; singers use their breath and their vocal cords but may disregard their arms, and so on.

By being aware of the entire body and not just the part you use to perform music, you start *involving* the entire body. You want to be aware of your legs if you are a violinist, your breath if you are a pianist, your shoulders if you are a trumpet player, your arms if you are a singer.

> ***All of you makes music, not just the parts that appear to be most important.***

The hosepipe – allow the flow

It is important to be as free as possible and to work with the body so that it is used at its greatest efficiency. By being physically free when you play or sing, you become a conduit for a powerful flow of energy that moves through your body. This becomes more than simply a physical freedom. This energy has within it the ability to inspire and move people. And surely this is what the role of music is? It is to inspire and move!

I often use an analogy of the hosepipe to describe how this energy flows through the body. Water can't flow freely through a hosepipe with kinks in it. Let's say you are sitting or standing, playing your instrument or singing. Imagine that a hosepipe full of rushing water is flowing through your body. The hosepipe must have no blockages, because if it does, the water comes out inconsistently, as either a rush or a trickle. Instead, it needs to come out in a focused form, through your hands if you are a string player or pianist, and equally through your hands, breath and embouchure if you are a wind or brass player and your breath and vocal cords if you are a singer.

Energy flow in action

You have been lying down on the floor, noticing where the aches and pains are in your body and focusing on letting them go. Now it is time to get up and be more active and to warm up your body further.

This next exercise, which comes from Tai Chi, is wonderful for getting the sense of being really connected to your whole body.

- Stand on the ground, feet hip-width apart and with flat shoes (or bare feet), and imagine roots growing out of your feet down into the ground deep into the centre of the earth.
- As the roots touch the centre of the earth, they draw energy back up through your feet, legs and torso, up through your shoulders and down your arms until it reaches your hands. (Singers: for hands, substitute neck, head and throat.)
- You then imagine a beach ball between your hands and allow the beach ball to lead you in any direction, but keeping your feet rooted to the floor.
- You might feel a tingling sensation between your fingers, which is simply the energy moving.

This gives you the feeling that you can move, but that the movement won't take you off course. From this point you can experiment with small fluid movements in your upper body, noticing that you can appear still and yet have an inner movement, all with a sense of being solidly connected to the ground.

Now cast your mind back to the body awareness exercise on the floor and then stand or sit with the understanding of these two exercises. You have tuned in to your body, you are aware of where you are holding tension, and you are able to begin letting go of it. You have fluidity in your body and an ability to move whilst keeping rooted to the ground, and you have a sense of energy in your upper body that has come from being grounded.

What does the flow feel like?

Before: shallow breathing, preoccupied by thoughts, unfocused, tired, tense, jittery	**After:** deep, expansive breathing, settled in the body, comfortably focused, relaxed but alert, free, calm

When you are connected to the flow of energy through your body, instead of feeling preoccupied, tense and resistant you are totally free and ready to go.

You are taking important steps towards preventing strain and keeping pain away.

- *Are you aware of the energy flow in your body?*
- *Have you ever noticed times and circumstances when it flowed better, or less well?*

- *Have you ever noticed that you can increase the flow?*

The dos and don'ts of sitting

However you perform, you are either going to be sitting or standing. This last exercise of being grounded is wonderful for singers and anyone playing an instrument standing, but you can also use the same exercise if you are sitting.

How you sit when playing your instrument is more important than you might first think, because playing-related injuries can often stem from an inefficient sitting position.

Your feet need to be flat on the floor so that you can be solid, stable and in as good alignment as is possible, drawing energy up from your imaginary centre of the Earth.

It is so easy to build up a habit, such as tucking your left foot under the chair, or lifting it partly off the floor, which doesn't help you in playing any better and can even be detrimental. Lifting your weight off the floor through your left foot for example, takes you off balance. You will be holding and lifting your arms to manage the lack of solidity under your feet. Similarly, wearing high heels throws your whole body out of alignment, meaning that you will be compensating for the different position.

It is best to sit on the front half of the stool or chair. This means that you support yourself from what I call your core – your abdominal muscles, where all your strength and power comes from. This is infinitely preferable to sitting further back, as if it were a comfortable armchair. By doing this, you are supporting yourself from your thighs, which are not so efficient at doing the job as your abdominal muscles when engaged.

Once you have a sense of the support of your core muscles, rock from side to side on your 'sit bones', the small bones in your bottom, and notice how this enables you to have freedom in your whole torso, if you should need it. Now sit as if you are growing out of your core, tall and upright, without holding yourself tight in any way, as the Alexander Technique would recommend.

When it comes to the piano, the height of the stool is really important. Contrary to popular opinion, it is not so much how tall you are but the length of your upper arm that matters when it comes to sitting at the right height. You are aiming to sit at the piano with your elbows approximately level with the keys or a maximum of 10-15% higher. This means that if your upper arm is on the short side, you will need to sit lower than if your upper arm is longer. I have a student who is the same height as me, and yet because she has longer upper arms than me, she needs to sit at the highest level that the stool can go, whereas I sit on the lowest.

Sitting at the wrong height, coupled with an inefficient sitting position, can cause all sorts of problems.

Jem came to me with shooting pains in his arms, wondering what he was doing wrong. With a quick glance I could see that he was sitting far too high, so that he was almost towering over the piano. He told me that the stool he used normally was a fixed height and that he had just got used to it. Changing the height he sat at made a very rapid difference, and his pain had diminished within a few days.

Sitting too high at the piano doesn't allow enough of the right contact with the keys. It is easy to put unnecessary strain on your upper arms. Equally, sitting too low can be a strain. If your arms are below the level of the keyboard then the simple act of moving your fingers and hands becomes more of an effort than it needs to be, because you are working against gravity.

For orchestral players, the equivalent is to make sure the music stand is at a comfortable height so that you are not straining in any way to see it. And if you are short-sighted and are craning your neck forward to see, it may simply be a case of moving the stand or getting suitable glasses!

Once you have found a way in which you can sit or stand with freedom, you notice the difference in the flow of your own energy. This brings us on to the concept of effortless power, well known to the world of martial arts: core stability.

Effortless power from core stability

A number of years ago, I took part in a Shiatsu course. Every day, we did some Tai Chi exercises as a warm up. One of the exercises had a profound effect on me and for the first time, all the loose ends regarding how to play with power, effortlessly, tied neatly together as I understood where our power comes from.

We were in pairs, with one partner standing opposite the other, elbows touching their waists and arms and hands straight out, palms facing upwards. This person was to try as hard as they could to hold their arms up against the other partner pushing down with all their force, and both were to notice what they felt doing this. My partner took the role of pushing first and I was the recipient. Within seconds, I felt my arms strain under the effort she was making, and we both staggered with the force. My arms hurt and so did hers.

The next stage in the exercise was for me as the recipient to focus on the area just underneath my navel, and feel it as the strong power base of my body, drawing energy up from the ground through my feet and my legs. I focused on this strength, letting go of my need to force my partner's hands up, and discovered to my amazement that she couldn't get anywhere near pushing my arms down. My arms felt solid and strong in a way that I had not experienced before.

I understood in my body that we have an ability to harness energy through our bodies in such a way that can be used in playing our instrument.

This understanding of core stability is important, and makes a significant difference when playing music. The power and strength needed to play can be free and effortless; there is no need to force. There are two good reasons why effortless power is better than force. First, it is good and healthy for the performer, meaning that one part of the body is not taking all the strain for playing and can share it out; second, the sound is always infinitely better.

What core stability feels like in the body

I had a student once who had been a principal ballerina in the Royal Ballet when she was younger. When I talked to her about core stability as it related to the piano, she understood immediately. She told me that as a ballet dancer, you had to be exceptionally strong in your legs and the whole region around the abdominal muscles, in order to support the upper body in being free.

If you go to a public space, such as a train station, in the West, and watch the way people walk, you will notice that Westerners generally walk from their upper bodies. Stiff, hunched shoulders, shallow breathing, rushing to get somewhere. It is as if we are led by our heads, and the rest of our bodies are only useful in as much as they carry our heads from one place to the next.

If you go to India, you will see something very different. The Indians walk from their core stability. All their energy is around their abdomen and lower back, and their upper body seems to float up and out from that. They walk slower and with enormous grace.

Pilates, a physical exercise system, which many ballet dancers have worked with, talks about the muscles around the centre of the body, that I call the core, or core stability, as the "powerhouse". All movement in Pilates begins in the powerhouse and flows outward to the rest of the body. As well as Pilates, you come across it in the martial arts, yoga and almost all sports. It is universal.

If you find it difficult to get a sense of these muscles, try this simple exercise. Pretend you are blowing up a balloon and you will find that you are engaging your core muscles.

For musicians, focusing on your core stability gives you a bigger perspective. It takes you away from being predominantly in your mind and brings you back into your body.

Essentially, it is about power coming from your belly rather than force coming from your muscles.

It helps you to stay physically freer. Your upper body will be freer if you put your focus on your core stability, your source of power.

Core stability and good use of sound

When I first explored the whole idea of playing from your core at the piano, I was amazed at the difference it made. I felt freer, more grounded. I was putting less emphasis on my hands and fingers and finding a wonderful support from the rest of my body. I hadn't realised that my whole body could enable me to get a rich, resonant sound from any dynamics I needed. There was no strain anymore, no need to push or try. I couldn't believe it was so easy!

Think about playing a loud chord on the piano. You may feel that you have to 'make' a loud sound, so your muscles tense and you push hard onto the keys. The sound that results is brittle and harsh. Now just by focusing on your core, allow the sound to flow up through your body, down through your arms and to your fingers, as if they were a hollow vessel. You will find that the sound is completely different. It is no longer brittle and harsh; it is rich and dynamic.

The sound has a resonance to it. It projects and it doesn't hurt the ears. And just as importantly, it doesn't hurt your hands!

It still amazes me that all that has to happen to find this remarkable energy that is available to all of us, is just to focus on it. Just by thinking of the power coming from our core, the sound changes and the power is there.

This applies to every instrument. You wouldn't grip a violin or a cello tightly and expect to create a rich, resonant sound. The instrument would rebel and would result in a strangled, tight sound. With any woodwind or brass instrument, you have to use your core muscles simply to make a good sound at all. Focusing on your embouchure and your fingers only, wouldn't get you very far at all. Likewise, as a singer, it is so much better to focus on your breathing and diaphragm supported by your core, taking the pressure away from all the activity in the throat and the neck. You can't get a rich, resonant sound unless you do this. It is as if the abdomen and the core muscles are the foundation and building blocks for every instrument. With those muscles engaged, you have more resources, more energy and more power.

- *Do you have a sense of where your 'core' is and how to engage the muscles?*
- *Are you able to get a clear sense of how your playing or singing improves if you play from your core?*

Gravity is free – use it!

You now have more of a physical and visceral understanding of the difference between power coming from your belly and force coming from your muscles. Gravity is another resource that can help us produce an effortless, resonant sound.

Gravity can support you in everything you do to make music. Rather than try hard to 'make' the movements needed to play your instrument or 'make' a sound, you can learn to work with, rather than against, gravity.

A string player can allow the weight of his bow arm to create a rich sound rather than forcing the bow on to the string. He can allow his fingers to fall onto the fingerboard, rather than push them there. A woodwind player, similarly, can allow his fingers to fall onto the keys.

A pianist can do the same, allowing the weight of her arm to provide the energy for a rich, resonant sound, rather than push the sound through force and effort.

Gravity needs to be used as a resource, along with finding your power centre in your core muscles. Using the two together releases an enormous power that makes playing the instrument or singing so much easier. It becomes almost effortless, and if everything is in alignment, your body working for you rather than against you, you will find that you have more energy than you knew was possible.

Freedom in the tiny movements

We have looked at how to flow energy up through the trunk of the body, but it doesn't stop at the hands. Freedom in playing is a fluidity that is made up of many small, free movements. Tension in playing is a locking down of all those small movements.

Building freedom into your playing is essential. But what is freedom in movement?

> *When you look at someone performing, what might appear to be free may in fact not be, and what might appear tense and held may in fact be very free.*

It is tempting to think that movement equals freedom, but people who move excessively can easily be compensating for excessive tension held elsewhere in their bodies; and people who appear very still aren't necessarily holding tension. There can be a form of movement and freedom within their stillness.

Sophie came to me with pains in her wrists and arms. She looked incredibly free when she played and it was clear how confusing it could appear to anyone who watched her. She had frequently had people saying to her that they didn't know why she had problems playing because she looked so free.

What was happening was that her outward, larger movements were free but underneath there were miniscule tightenings in her arms and hands. It was as if you needed a metaphorical magnifying glass to see it because it wasn't visible to the naked eye.

When I did observe her closely, I could see these tiny movements that were always held and always tense.

I demonstrated what she was doing by showing her the tense version followed by the free version, and then spent most of the session showing her how she could let go in each one of the tiny movements.

Efficiency of physical energy

When you are doing something as complex as playing a musical instrument, there is a need to be as efficient as possible with the movements you use. It is easy to give away precious physical energy on movements that are rigid and tense, and that aren't helping you with the task in hand.

I have often seen pianists struggle to play a passage that they should be able to play with ease, and when I look closely I see a hand that is so tight and gripped that the tendons are standing out. The hand needs to be as elastic as possible. You need to be able to stretch it and then immediately release it back into a free position. Stretch an elastic band too tight and it snaps. The hand is not much different.

Most tension in the hands comes from being in an outstretched position, as an unconscious desire to avoid mistakes as well as to prepare and be ready for what is next. But it is really a case of dealing with what is here and now. Right now in this moment you need to be free in this small movement. Then you move to the next movement and stay free. You may have a miniscule bit of strain whilst you move from one movement to the next, but you don't keep that strain. This way of doing things means you may have 1% of strain in any one movement, compared to 99% of strain when you keep the movement locked to prepare for the next.

The same principle applies to moving your finger from one note to the next in large stretches. Your fingers can't manage large stretches with an outstretched hand because everything seizes up. But if each time you move to the next note, you return your hand to a free, neutral position, your hand is free at every point. This is how your hand can be like an elastic band. I call this 'the point of gravity'.

All your energy and power is behind that one note, moving to the point of gravity, and it is not dispersed out in a tense, outstretched hand.

This can apply to most instruments. A string player, putting his fingers on the finger board, can remind himself to stay free after a big stretch, and if the stretch has to be maintained, to free up within that stretch. Clarinettists, who might find certain fingering positions slightly uncomfortable, need to remember to relax their hands and fingers over those positions.

Pianists often say to me that they struggle to play big chords and that their arms tighten up when they do. They will say that it must be because they have small hands and find the stretch a challenge. But I show them how small my hands are and that I can still manage to play large chords with freedom.

The secret is in keeping the strain part of the movement to an absolute minimum and the freedom to a maximum. If you play big chords on the piano and that is a big stretch for you, you start by approaching the stretch, with a split second amount of strain and then as soon as you land on the chord you free up your whole hand. You don't keep it in a state of tension for even nano-second longer than is necessary.

Be aware of the thumb!

The thumb can be a real culprit for so many instrumentalists. The thumb is extremely strong. It is normally used for grasping and balancing out against the other fingers. If you pick up a mug, you do it with the balance of your thumb on one side and the fingers on the other. But for a musician, your thumb will have a very specific role depending on the instrument.

Jim was a pianist who was also an oboe player. On one occasion, I noticed that his left thumb was locked and tight when he played the piano, but that his right thumb wasn't. It suddenly occurred to me that it might be something to do with the way he played the oboe. Fortunately, he had his oboe with him and I asked him to get it out so I could see how he played. And there it was! His left thumb was locked into position. By looking a bit more closely, I realised that it was the left thumb that was in effect holding the oboe up. I talked to him about it and he agreed that he had felt this need to hold the oboe up and realised that was why he was tensing his left thumb. But you don't need to tense muscles to lift something.

To explain this, I asked him to lift up the piano stool with very tense arms. He did and found it quite an effort. I asked him then to lift the piano stool with free, flexible arms, which he found considerably easier. This confirmed to him that having a tense thumb on the oboe was not helping him and that by keeping it completely free, he was able to keep the instrument supported with energy to spare. And he could also play the piano with greater freedom!

The thumb has a tendency to lock and therefore inhibit movement.

A violinist who locks her left thumb round the neck of the violin will massively restrict her ability to play with freedom. But it doesn't have to be obvious to cause a problem. Even a very small amount of tension can cause a problem, leading back to the wrist, elbow and shoulder.

An important hinge joint

The wrist is another big culprit in causing aches and pains. It is so easy to keep it locked. On the piano, it is essential that it is free.

Most of the tendonitis problems I have seen over the years have stemmed from a locked wrist.

This is because pianists unconsciously think that they have to 'make' their fingers work, and this forced effort can lock the wrist in seconds. Without knowing the importance of the wrist in all its different movements – lateral, vertical, circular – a pianist can lock down their wrist, and restrict their ability to play.

The wrist needs to be free for string players, but woodwind and brass players may not see the relevance to them. You may not need to use your wrist in the same way that a pianist might, but it is just as important that it is not locked and held in place. You still have to move your fingers and your wrist is connected to your fingers. One tense spot in the body will affect everything else. Our whole body needs to be in alignment to work efficiently.

- *Are you able to pinpoint tense spots like thumbs, wrists and cheeks, and see if you notice how they are blocking the flow of energy?*

Summary

In this chapter we have looked at how pain can occur through tension and blocked energy, and we have considered ways of allowing energy to flow freely, powerfully and effortlessly. Here are some steps you can take if you need help with this.

- *The first step* is to use the simple exercises mentioned to become aware of the flow of energy through the whole body, where it is blocked by tension and how to increase the flow.

- *The second step* is to make sure the way you sit or stand is not inhibiting your energy flow.

- *The third step* is to focus on your core and bring your sound up from that, sensing the way it comes effortlessly.

- *The fourth step* is to make sure your energy flow is not being blocked by hands, faces and wrists.

With a handle on the pain and free-flowing energy, you can really sense what playing to the peak of your ability is all about.

In the next chapter we will look at how to practise well and efficiently, so that you have a profound knowledge of your instrument and the music you are playing. I've called it the art of practising.

8

The art of practising

What I have achieved by industry and practice, anyone else with tolerable natural gift and ability can also achieve.

J S Bach

Jake was practising five hours a day when he first started lessons with me. I had assumed he was practising for around an hour a day from the way he played. He was making 'some' progress but not an enormous amount. I was amazed when he told me how much time he was putting in. It didn't add up. So I asked him to give me an idea of exactly what he did in his five hours of allocated practice time. He was embarrassed and rather vague. A picture of endless repetition with no clear goals began to emerge, and it then dawned on me that although he was putting in the hours, he really didn't know how to practise.

Practising is a musician's food. We need it on a daily basis. It is our contact with our instrument and our living relationship with our instrument. Practising is a set of skills that need to be honed and refined over years to produce the results needed.

It is not just about practising itself; it is about how you practise and the quality of that practice.

Many a talented musician has fallen by the wayside through not knowing how to practise well and efficiently.

A musician who doesn't practise effectively is leaving too much to chance, and there is the strong risk that whatever talent they might have will not be evident. A talented, top-level performing musician would lose their position at the top if they stopped practising.

Hannah's helpful mother

Someone who practises well has usually been shown what to do from an early age.

Hannah told me that her mother had sat next to her from the age of six, encouraging her, helping her to learn her notes through a system of colours, and get her bowing right with nursery rhymes. It was fun, Hannah told me, and she couldn't wait to get to the cello every day.

As she got older, her mother still practised with her, making sure she was doing what her teacher had set her during the lesson. She showed her how to learn a whole piece and not just the first few bars, and how to feel really secure with what she was playing. This was done on a daily basis, until Hannah was confident enough to practise on her own.

Because she had started off with so much fun, enjoyment and support, the precedent had been set, and practising in Hannah's mind was positive and a normal part of the day.

Hannah was lucky to have both a teacher and a mother who could support her and help her build good habits. What she had was a foundation for a good relationship with practising.

Shining the spotlight on your practising

It is so easy to go into denial about practising. "Yes, I have practised. Of course I can play this passage. That will do. I need to get on with something else. I am sure that is good enough…" We can play such games with ourselves and all that is really happening is that we are deceiving ourselves.

It is critical to be able to shine a spotlight on the effectiveness of our practising. We need to be honest with each bar and then each phrase, each section and each piece. Do I really know it? What do I need to do to secure it further? Is this passage going to crumble under the pressure of the performance?

It can be difficult and awkward to take the lid off and really expose the way we practise.

We might fear that taking the lid off will expose a can of worms, or we may fear being exposed as a fraud who doesn't know what they are doing. Our games can be an unconscious way of hiding from that perceived threat of exposure.

"If I don't learn this properly, then if I don't play it well, I can say I didn't practise enough." The fear is that if we practise really well, then the performance we give shows us for who we are, and if we screw up at that, we will expose ourselves as frauds. So it is easier to back out in the first place. Or to say "I would rather just sight-read that because then I can blame any flaws on the fact that I never had a chance to practise it properly."

126

Over-practising

As much as we can go into denial with whether we are doing enough practising, we can equally play games with over-practising. Too much practising can come from an over-cultivated sense of duty. It is only too easy to put in six hours practise in a day, but in reality for that time not to be well used. It could have achieved everything we needed to in three, with most of the achievement being in the first hour! Those next few hours can so easily be wasted by simply not being engaged.

Over-practising can also come from being too anxious about playing 'perfectly' and not making mistakes. It is then the fear that drives the practising and not the joy.

But music needs to be a joyful experience, and the desperation that comes from having to get it right at all costs can take away the enjoyment of the experience.

Similarly, we need regular breaks. We can't concentrate effectively for so many hours without breaks, and our bodies may start complaining. Breathing, stretching and having something to eat or drink all help keep our efficiency levels high, mentally and physically.

Debunking the myths about practising

There are always musicians around who don't appear to need to practise. They may practise less than other people but still manage to play fantastically as if they know their music very thoroughly. It is so easy to think that they are somehow more talented than everyone else and that they just don't need to practise. But they do.

What is probably happening is that they are exceptionally efficient and effective with their practising, so what takes one person three hours, takes them one hour.

Mozart is commonly seen to be a composer who is simply a 'genius'. At the age of five, he was suddenly able to compose little pieces, and that this must just mean that he was more talented than a normal five year old. Obviously he had exceptional talent, but what is not often mentioned is that by his sixth birthday, it is estimated that Mozart had studied 3,500 hours of music with his father, the teacher and well-known violinist, Leopold Mozart. *Genius Explained* by Dr Michael Howe of Exeter University.

There is so much you can do with effective practising. I have come across young students who don't appear to be particularly talented, and yet they immerse themselves in music, practise effectively, and over time emerge into very fine musicians.

Building the skill base

There is an aspect of practising that is very practical. It is a case of building the skill base. If you perform a piece of music, you have to know it. You have to know it deeply and intimately in a way that means that that you are secure enough to perform it and not be thrown off course by any nerves and adrenalin you may have. It means being secure enough to let go and express the music.

Practising can often be misunderstood. It is not fiddling around with the music aimlessly and playing the tunes you like one after the other. Nor is it doing what young children often do by playing the beginning over and over again but never getting much further. It is much more gritty than that.

Practising doesn't entertain, nor should it be easy on the ear.

If practising is too pleasant to listen to, something is not quite right. I remember talking to some people who had once lived next door to the cellist, Rostropovich. They told me that it wasn't much fun listening to him practise because they never heard him play any whole pieces of music, just lots of little bits over and over again. They were clearly rather disappointed. But this is part of what practising is. Practising is about taking the music apart and putting it back together again, with a far deeper knowledge than you had before you started.

Learning how to practise well is learning a complex set of skills which can take years to build up. Practising is rarely taught, and many potentially good musicians drop by the wayside because they don't know how to practise well and efficiently. What is often taught at the early stages is just to get the notes right through repetition. But that is only half of the story. Repetition is crucial, but not for its own sake.

What is needed is repetition with intent, clarity, strategy and efficiency.

There are different stages to practising which you may know consciously or unconsciously.

You start by getting the big picture. You need to know what you're dealing with, to acquaint yourself with the territory. This may be a case of listening to the piece with a score or of sight-reading what you can. I often take scores on the train, poring over them, getting a sense of what I am dealing with, working out where I will start. You need to have a context for doing the work.

The next stage is breaking it down into small sections, exploring, building a mental picture of what you are doing, making mistakes, learning what not to do because of those mistakes. You might memorise sections, check yourself for what you know and what you don't know and starting to knit it all together. This all needs extraordinary honesty.

You need to shine a spotlight on what you are doing and make sure you really do know a section rather than pull the wool over your own eyes, and leave it with the unconscious thought that it will be all right when you play it. It won't!

That is the time when the bits you don't know can whip up your nerves into a frenzy. It is best to shine the spotlight on your playing in the privacy of your own practice room than in the concert hall.

Sometimes that is easier said than done. I remember preparing for a concert with two singers. Half an hour before the performance, one of the singers decided to change one of the songs he was singing because he didn't think he could manage one of the top notes. So I was suddenly in the position of having to prepare a song in half an hour. I didn't have the courage at the time to confront this well-known singer and say that I wasn't happy to learn a song in such a short time, just before the concert. For me it was just as unpleasant to be put in that position as it was for him to deal with a top note he wasn't happy about. I did what I could in the time I had. My sight-reading is good and I learn fast; I just prayed that I could get away with it.

The moment I walked on stage, it was as if everything I *didn't* know about that song was suddenly looming large in front of my eyes. My nerves jumped into a gear that was very unpleasant, and I felt extraordinarily insecure. I managed it, but it was a deeply uncomfortable experience and a case of surviving. There was no time and space to be expressive, to communicate with the audience. I was just hanging on in there, somehow. I decided at that point that I would never go on to the concert platform unprepared; it simply wasn't worth it!

Tortoises and hares

One of the key things about practising is not to be in a hurry. You need patience and you need to be prepared to go slow. By taking a piece apart and working at sections slowly, you get to know them deeply and intimately. You need to sort out your mistakes, check your precision and really understand every last detail. The slow, thorough, methodical approach is what will enable you to have the security you need.

The tortoise moves slowly and with intent. The hare bounds all over the place, seemingly much faster but not knowing where he is going. Despite the hare's speed, the tortoise wins. And it is the same with practising.

The musician who practises in detail with patience will win out over the musician who just wants to play the bits he knows and hope for the best with all the rest of it.

Have you ever wondered how someone can learn a concerto in a mere three weeks, and learn it well? It is because they have honed their practising skills to a very fine degree. They don't have more talent than other people, they simply know how to practise very, very efficiently. This is the kind of high quality work that leaves you tired at the end of an hour but very fulfilled.

Once you know what this kind of work is, and you build it in to your physiology, you will find you can't do without it. It becomes a vital part of your everyday routine. Not only that, but it *needs* to be part of your everyday routine. Even letting go of a practising routine for a few days has an impact. Vladmir Horowitz once said "If I skip practice for one day, I notice. If I skip practice for two days, my wife notices it. If I skip practice for three days, the world notices it."

- *What is your relationship with practising?*
- *Is it a chore that has to be got through, or is it a fulfilling part of your life?*
- *Do you feel that you are practising effectively?*
- *Can you sense that practising could be an 'art'?*
- *To what degree do you feel it is an art for you?*

A basic template for practising

Practising needs to be done with intent and with a strategy. This is a very basic template that you can use to check you are practising thoroughly at the beginning stages of getting to know a piece.

- First you need to get to the stage when you can play a whole piece or a large section of a piece *slowly* and with the fundamentals of notes, fingerings, dynamics and articulation in place.
- Then take either two bars or four bars of music and give yourself

a mini goal of playing it say, three times, looking at the music. During this playing, you are engaging entirely with the music, checking you know everything very thoroughly.

- You then tell yourself that after these three times of playing with the music open in front of you, you are going to put the music on one side, and play without it. This is an extra incentive and should keep you focused when you are getting to know it with the music those first few times.

- When you get to the point where you play without the music, let go and see what happens. It might be accurate or it might not. If you can't remember something, open your eyes and check with the music, so that you don't build anything in that is not accurate.

- Then try it again, always staying alert and engaged with the process.

- Once you can play those few bars without the music, give yourself the next mini goal, which is to play with your eyes shut. This adds more complexity into the process, demanding that you let go of any visual cues and rely entirely on the physicality and your ears.

- The next step is to do the same to the following few bars, and then add the two together. You continue adding more and more sections, never leaving it until you know it on a very deep level. Once you have done this, play the extract through with the music and see how easy it feels.

Always be honest when you practise. Do you *really* know this section? Could you play it in your sleep? Are you kidding yourself that you know it when in fact it is only fifty per cent there?

Be completely comfortable with whatever you are doing at each stage of learning. You need to be completely in control and make sure that you are never pushing yourself to be ahead or further along than you actually are. Always remember to connect all the small sections together and play whole chunks of the piece through to see where you are up to.

This way of working may seem painstaking at the beginning, but you will find you get faster and faster and more and more efficient if you stick with it. You will also have the immense satisfaction of knowing a piece of music extremely well.

It may sound obvious, but when I have taken a student through this process and they have really understood and integrated it, their playing leaps forward in an impressive way. Their whole approach to learning changes and they become more independent.

It is worth mentioning at this stage that sticking with your practice when it gets really difficult is essential. If something feels difficult, it is because new neural pathways are being formed in the brain for the very purpose of learning something new. Giving up when it gets difficult means you won't learn!

Keep your creativity when you practise

Bear in mind, however, that the steps I've listed above are a template and a template only. Don't in any way feel restricted by this, as if your practising and performing depended on it. It would be like religiously following a map when you are going on a walk. Of course you need to know where you are going, and the map can be very useful in giving you those indicators. But what if you suddenly decide to explore a grassy bank that appears to be calling you? And what about the country pub you see signposted that is off the main track? Maybe you decide to follow the path to the pub and go back on a different route. The map has been useful, but if it restricts you, it restricts your walk. Likewise, if you are too rigid in your practising, you won't be able to play the music with freedom and expression when it comes to the concert.

Having a method for practising is essential for covering your bases, for knowing where you are and what you are doing. Then open the door and let curiosity and spontaneity come in. At every stage, explore, discover, change your mind. If you suddenly feel weary of a certain piece, change it and play something else. You might be in the middle of the four- bar phrase that you are securing, all is going well, but you decide you want to put it in context.

"Can I play it with the first sixteen bars I have just learned?"

"Today, I will not put the dynamics in because I have too much to think about."

"Maybe this time, I will play it slowly so that I have time to take notice of my breathing, check how my body feels, check my shoulders are free and my wrist is flexible."

"How do I feel about this? Am I loving this music or have I switched off and gone into auto pilot?"

This not only gives the methodological part of your mind a rest, but it also keeps you fresh with the enjoyment of what you are doing.

Curiosity and fascination

Practising needs to be something that we relish, at least in part, otherwise it can become a chore that has to be done. At every stage, we need to remind ourselves that we are playing music because we love it and because we love the music that we play. Why else would we do it? Our love for the instrument and music then starts to fuel the desire to build up a skill-base, which in turn enables us to play well and with full expression.

Out of that love comes an approach which differs from duty. It is curiosity and fascination.

If we approach our practising with these qualities, we become engrossed and engaged in what we are doing, and much more likely to achieve. We become curious about everything.

Curiosity requires openness. If we explore, anything could come across our way. We need to be open and discerning about what we are doing.

Free control

There is a particular state of performing which I call 'free control'. It is when you have both the control and the freedom. This type of control is not something that is restrictive or limited, but a way of ordering the material. Within that you have freedom. This is the absolute ideal of performing and once you have found it, you will always want to perform that way.

Vicky was a piano student of mine who was struggling with a particularly difficult passage. We broke it down, taking it apart to see exactly how it needed to be played, working at it slowly until she really understood its inner architecture. But she couldn't let go and simply play it. She was trying to hang on to it, to control it in some way. So I suggested she throw caution to the wind and play it any old how, knowing that if it all fell apart she could deal with that later. She did exactly that. She just played it with abandon, and then looked at me with amazement at the results: she had played it completely fluently!

By doing the work and then letting go, Vicky was able to play with a proficiency she didn't know she had.

Neither one is enough without the other. You can't just do the control because it doesn't have the space. It becomes a technical exercise and often there is tension within it. Nor can you throw caution to the wind and hope for the best. You need to do the work, know exactly what you are doing and by letting go, you find the real type of control – free control. The great jazz saxophonist and composer, Charlie Parker, brilliantly summed this up when he said "You've got to learn your instrument. Then, you practise, practise, practise. And then, when you finally get up there on the bandstand, forget all that and just wail."

- *Have you had the experience of 'free control'?*
- *How did it feel?*
- *Were you able to congratulate yourself for achieving it, if you did?*

Being in the present moment

When we practise, we prepare for a performance. We have looked at some methods of practising which can help build the security needed to perform, but there are times when practising isn't a controlled exercise. It is messy, uncertain and yet through that there is space for us to explore, to be curious, fascinated. Practising that is too ordered runs the risk of becoming an ordered performance.

We need to practise our ability to be in the moment, to be fully alive, our spontaneity.

Being in the present moment and being fully engaged is one of the most important aspects of both practising and performing.

I remember travelling to India and spending two weeks in a small seaside village in Kerala. The sense of time I noticed there was much freer than Western time. Appointments were free and relaxed and not bound by so many restrictions. When I would ask what time something needed to be done, I was invariably told "Indian time" with a big smile. After some days, getting to know the way the Indians lived their lives, I found myself picking up, as if by osmosis, the ability simply to "be".

I didn't notice it when I was there, but when I came back to England, I had the extraordinary experience of being able to get out of my head and to engage fully with the present moment. I found myself walking in the countryside, engrossed by a leaf on a tree or the patterns on the tree trunk, not listing my experience in my head and making some form of mental comment. In fact, there was no chatter and no commentary going on at all. I was simply "being". I was then able to take that "engagement" and apply it to mundane activities, such as doing the washing up. I wasn't thinking, I was simply washing up – feeling the water, hearing the sounds of the clanking plates. I was neither in the past or the future, only in the present.

When I was first back home, I could do this for about twenty minutes at a time. Finding myself going back to the mental commentary again was almost painful. It felt effortful and forced, and engaging in the moment was all that mattered. It was an extraordinary experience. After a period of time I started losing my daily experience of it, but I found that I had a new understanding of how to perform.

'Being present' is exactly what playing music is all about. When we are on the concert platform, we need to be absolutely present to the music in order to express it and project that expression.

Our mental activity lessens and we go into a space of total relaxed focus where the magic can happen.

Having an awareness of this is important for practising. It means that you can be more conscious of where you want to be and can then prepare for it. The preparation needs to be about more than getting the notes in the right places, interpreting the composer's style. It needs to include this sense of being in the present moment. Being in the present moment can only happen when everything is in place, totally secure and when you can let go and focus.

Being in the present moment is letting go of our chatty minds telling us what is going on and what we should think. If we let ourselves get bored, we switch into autopilot and our minds will chatter about whatever is attracting them in that moment. It could look something like this:

"Ok, I need to look at this section... I wish someone would shut that door to stop it banging... Oh no, I forgot to email that person about the concert next month... I hope it won't matter... I'm really hungry... I might have to go out in a minute to grab some chocolate... My phone is going... Shall I answer it?... I'd better get on with some work... Finding it difficult to concentrate..."

It is a case of consciously deciding to stop the mental chatter and come back to the music. Notice that your mind is chatting and instead of getting cross and frustrated with yourself, come back gently. Find something that you enjoy and let yourself become involved with it, fascinated and curious. What you are aiming at is to practise with presence and focus.

Learning how to let go of the chatty mind and being present in your practising is what you want to cultivate so that you can be fully in the present moment on stage.

So instead of being distracted – *"I wish that man would stop rattling his programme on the front row... I wonder whether my friends are here tonight... They said they would come but I didn't see them when I walked on..."* – you are fully present. The chat starts to subside, and you are absorbed in the music, completely. Your mind is there, but it is as if it is lightly touching your playing – bits of guidance for memory, structure, knowing where you are. It is a very different experience and much more enjoyable!

Sensory awareness

Have you ever pretended you were blind and have someone lead you by the arm? It is an extraordinary experience. You inevitably feel dependent, insecure and wobbly, but once you have let go of that aspect to it, you can relax into the senses.

Because we are so dependent on our sight, all the other senses that can easily be neglected bounce up to the surface once we don't have it.

If you go outside, you will start hearing sounds in ways that you might easily have ignored before. Sounds of cars and exactly where they are in relation to you, your own footsteps on the pavement, people's voices coming towards you and away from you. If you are in the countryside you will hear the birds, and your spatial awareness comes into sharp focus. You listen in a way that is highlighted and probably very unfamiliar.

Now take that experience to your instrument. Pretend for a short while that you are blind. You decide to play a note and because you have no visual distractions, you are able to hear the note finding its place in the space around you. The sound bounces off the wall and then back to you again. You hadn't noticed this before. Your spatial awareness in listening has just increased massively, and you are listening in a different, possibly unfamiliar way.

This time play a note and check in to how you feel. Feel the contact of the bow on the string, the feeling of the valves under your fingers, how your lips feel when you make a sound on your reed or the feeling of your sung sound resonating round your head. Your eyes are shut, you are listening and you are feeling. You are in a heightened state of awareness.

Now experiment with being with your instrument, looking at it with fresh eyes as if you had been blind all your life and you had suddenly been given back your sight. You see the sharpness and clarity of your edge of the bow or the gleaming brass that is now reflecting the light. Your eyes bask, simply enjoying the sensation of seeing.

Opening yourself up to this level of sensory awareness is very powerful. It supports you in being in the present moment, fully alert and alive, playing with total engagement with the music you are playing. Sensory engagement is the vessel through which the inspiration can flow.

Summary

We have looked at the art of practising and seen that it is a combination of honing your technical skills along with how you set yourself up so that you are best able to let the music flow. Here are some suggested steps to guide your practice.

- **The first step** is to be honest with yourself about the way you practise. Are you cutting corners, or over doing it, and could you do it more efficiently?

- **The second step** is to notice which parts of the music you need to take apart, repeat over and over, and then put it back together again.

- **The third step** is to experiment with free control and sensory awareness in the present moment, to see if you can see things with a fresh perspective.

In this chapter we have taken the concept of practice and broken it down into different aspects. We've looked at making it focused and efficient so that it supports what you do when you perform.

In the final chapter we will see how we become 'fertile ground' for the magic and power of musical inspiration to flow through.

9

Music from the inside out

This book has been about how you can clear away everything that is getting in the way of you performing to your peak. It is about clearing clutter on a physical, mental and emotional level. And then going to the next stage of allowing the freedom you need on all of those levels.

So why is it important to find this freedom, physically, mentally and emotionally?

Let it flow

Finding physical freedom is important, not only for managing technical playing challenges and for maintaining the health and well-being of your body, but also because it allows a physical channel for your emotional expression.

When I have encouraged a musician to free up physically, it is almost automatic that their expression frees up as well.

It doesn't always happen straight away because sometimes they have to take time to get into a different gear. By being tense, all their energy goes into holding that tension and trying desperately to express themselves somehow. There is no energy left over and their own natural and unique expression is suffocated; it doesn't have a chance. When they let go and start the process of releasing held tension, it can feel a relief and strangely freeing. There is no 'doing' or 'trying', it is simply letting it happen. It is a case of 'allowing' the expression to come through them, and allowing is a completely different experience. This can be very new and very unfamiliar for musicians who have been holding their tension for a long time.

Amy was a case in point. She had spent a couple of years beating herself up, struggling with a very low self-esteem, and this had translated partially into very stiff hands and a limited technique. Whenever I showed her a newer, freer way of doing something, she would get frustrated with herself because she couldn't do it straight away, and would always come back with, "But I am trying to do it!" And her hands would stay stiff, and her technique wouldn't change.

At a certain point, all the work we had done on shifting the Inner Critic started to sink in and Amy started to show signs of changing. She was no longer beating herself up, her hands were freeing up and she could manage more technical challenges than she had ever imagined were possible.

She had arrived at the point of freedom from the physical and emotional clutter that had held her back for so long. I asked her what it felt like. "It's so much easier to play and it is so much more fun," was her response.

And this was just the beginning. She hadn't even started to discover the full degree of her expressive qualities, and I knew that given time and the desire for it, this could start flowing.

Performing music demands that not only are you free of physical blockages, but that you are also free of emotional blockages. But you are very unlikely to have been taught this as part of your general or even musical education. Learning how to think, remembering facts and how to develop skills will have been considered much more important, and how you deal with your emotions won't have been part of the curriculum. But if you are a musician you need to be able to express yourself. You can learn this up to a point, but to be able to express yourself fully means in the first instance that you need to be free from anything that blocks you or numbs you emotionally.

There is so much that can throw you off course: not owning your own motivation, hanging on to a story of how badly you have been treated without finding your own means of moving through it, being run by your Inner Critic and performance anxiety that paralyses you on the stage. So much emotional energy can be wasted on all this and all our insecurities! But put the other way round, once you release that emotional energy, there is so much space for your own unique expression to come forth.

Heartfelt expression

Music has to come from the heart, and it is the heart-felt expression that touches anyone listening to music. I have been to performances which have been impressive but I have been left cold. Sometimes I can't put my finger on why a performance hasn't touched me, but I walk away without having shared anything from the musician who has performed. Other times,

I have been moved to tears by a student's performance in my own studio. It may not be flawless in the way it is played, but if that person has opened themselves emotionally, it can touch very deeply. It is how responsive the performer is to his or her own heart and soul that makes the difference.

An ability to play stylistically, expressively and technically is, of course, essential, but if the connection with the heart and soul is absent, then however wonderfully played it might be, there is an emptiness to the performance. It is an opportunity missed.

Sometimes we can be overrun by all sorts of painful emotions that swirl inside us. Directing emotions such as anger and grief out from inside us and into music is wonderfully freeing and much healthier for us than bottling it up. All too often these painful emotions get pushed down for safety's sake because it may not feel safe to look at them, or we feel we don't have the time or the know-how to face them. This just serves to compound the problem. Pushing uncomfortable feelings inwards numbs us and halts our ability to express freely.

Strong emotions, no matter whether it is happiness, grief, or rage, can actually be used to *open* our channels of expression. It is through our emotions and our feelings that we feel alive. We may not like them or find them easy to deal with, but they can be expressed and transformed through playing, bringing a powerful, moving quality to our performance and practising. They can be given a meaning and a value. They open us up and enable us to feel the fire and the flow which moves us and moves our audience.

I remember going to a concert that a friend, Linda, gave. I knew that she was going through an enormous amount of emotional pain; one of her best friends had died in a car accident the week before and I was wondering whether she would cancel the concert. She decided to go ahead with the concert, dedicating it to her friend. That concert was extraordinary. I could feel the pain she was feeling and I could also see, hear and feel how she was channelling it into the music. Her performing was profound, open, expressive and very moving. Her playing had a depth and an emotional openness that was more than normal. She was given a standing ovation at the end and the audience were clearly moved. Linda told me, sometime later, that she had found the concert extremely cathartic and was pleased that she had gone ahead with it at such a difficult time.

Playing out emotions like this can be transformational. It takes the pain and directs it into expression. In the process of doing this, both the performer and the audience can be touched on a very deep level. An amazing creativity and beauty can come from feelings that are this uncomfortable.

These painful feelings need to be distinguished from the negative feelings connected to the Inner Critic, which are destructive, limiting and blocking. It is not that you *want* to have painful feelings, it is just that if you have them, you have the choice to transform them. You can channel them into music and transform yourself and your audience in the process. Ideally you want to lift yourself into a good-feeling place where your expression can flow freely.

- *Have you ever experienced the transformation of painful or bitter feelings into something beautiful and universal?*
- *Were you aware of a sense of openness that allowed the feelings to flow?*

Connecting to your good feelings

In Chapter 5, on managing your nerves, we saw how you can put yourself in your bubble so that you feel safe and protected. You then fill the bubble with anything that makes you feel good. If your painful feelings are detracting from rather than adding to your performance or practice, then making a choice to have good feelings is extraordinarily powerful and has an incredible impact on how you perform. These 'feel-good' triggers don't need to be big and important; they just need to be things that help you get into a good-feeling place. It can be as simple as allowing yourself to fall in love with the music you are playing, or remembering a fun-filled day with friends. It is by connecting to your good feeling place that you can connect to your inspiration.

Good feelings and MP3 players

You can then take this whole exercise to another level. Start by taking yourself to that good-feeling place. Let's say that imagining yourself walking on the beach lifts you up there. Whenever you think about walking on the beach, you feel fantastic, free, alive and fully yourself. You can actually do something very practical that takes you one step further than your imagination and really build the feelings in. Go to a beach and walk along it. Love it, feel fantastic and take the music you are learning for a particular concert on your phone. Play that music as you are walking along the beach and build in the connections between the music and your good-feeling place. Then, when you come back to your practice room, you have something more tangible to connect to. You have started, in a more conscious and tangible way, to connect the music you are playing to your endorphins.

Rick was a fantastic performer and had come to me with a well-prepared Beethoven sonata. He was playing it extremely well already and I was curious to see whether his playing could be improved even further by connecting to a good-feeling place and relating that to the music. I asked him to imagine something that really lit him up. For him, it was the feeling of going out on a boat with his friends on a hot summer's day. So I asked him to feel that as intensely as he could and then immediately play the first movement of the sonata. I was bowled over by what I heard. His playing had changed. It was even freer and it was inspired. Somehow those good feelings had opened him up further and a magic was flowing through him. I had a lump in my throat from the sheer intensity of his expression.

The interconnectedness of music and life

The great, classical composers were equally inspired by the world around them. Many of them relished being in nature, absorbing what it offered them. Beethoven was one of those who went for long walks in the countryside, allowing himself to be inspired and then feeding his compositions with that inspiration.

I found it inspirational to see how something so simple could have such a profound impact on a musician's means of expression. It made me think that we are all capable of so much, if we can find the key to unlock us. It also shows how interconnected we are. Learning and performing music is connected to our life.

In no way can music be put in a compartment and separated off from everything we experience in our life, our hopes, our dreams, what inspires us, our love affairs, friendships and our whole inner emotional landscape.

I have worked with adults who have relished learning the piano again after many years of focusing on their career or family, and they find that what they learn about the instrument and music has a direct knock-on effect to their life. A dentist once told me that learning to free up her right arm, in order to play more freely on the piano, had enabled her to grip with less unnecessary tension on her dentist's drill! She also noticed that she was less tired after a day's work because she was generally less tense. A businessman discovered that his golf swing had improved massively over the period of time he had taken up piano lessons again. He had learned to be freer in his piano playing and this had impacted his golf!

One of my favourite examples of how the learning and performing of music can impact different aspects of your life connects to a young surgeon.

The work I did with Hiran over a period of a year or more was directly connected to his work as a surgeon. His Inner Critic was strong in him and came out particularly strongly when he played the piano. He was aware that he didn't have time to practise much, and therefore wasn't playing as he knew he could. I saw his Inner Critic paralyse his ability to play, and how his hands tensed up as a result.

We talked about how that could also impact his work as a surgeon; if his hands tensed up when he was being very self- critical at the piano, it followed that the same would happen when he was in the operating theatre. Likewise, the anxiety he felt when performing on the piano also directly related to his performing in theatre. I showed him how he could transform the Inner Critic and calm his nerves through the piano, and he took each lesson with him to his work.

After time, he found that he was reassuring himself during an operation and reminding himself to stay calm. He stopped allowing himself to feel insecure by unhelpful remarks at critically important times from other people around him, and he began to find a calm focus in his work. He began to realise that not only was he not being affected by other people's anxiety, but that his increasingly calm focus was having an impact on the people around him. His newfound management of his emotions was radiating outwards in a positive way. Hiran's work started improving and started to be recognised. He was en route to becoming an extremely good, caring and successful surgeon.

What was intriguing for me was that this also worked in reverse. What he discovered through managing his emotions and Inner Critic in the operating theatre then translated back again into his work at the piano, and his playing started to improve noticeably. He showed me how much of what we do in our lives is interconnected.

Music: a process of co-operation

There are three main components in the performance of classical music: the composer, the performer and the audience. If one of these is missing, the whole structure falters. The composer's role is essential, as is the performer's. Without a performer, the music is only dots on a piece of paper, possibly interesting but not what it was originally intended for. Without a composer, the performer has nothing to play. The only one that can survive without one of the components, is the performer without the audience. As a performer, you can play the composer's music to yourself and there can still be enjoyment from it. Find an audience, though, and the dynamic changes.

It is a process of co-operation; the composer creates, the performer re-creates and expresses, and the audience receives.

There is a curious dynamic that operates when musicians perform in front of an audience. The musician comes out on to the stage and needs to take responsibility for the performance immediately, showing that he is in control even if he feels extremely nervous. The audience doesn't want to see a performer wobble or show discomfort; it is too uncomfortable. Once the performer has started playing with this sense of responsibility, the audience can relax, and this then carries energetically to the performer, who can also relax. The performer still carries the responsibility of focusing and expressing, and the audience needs to be open, receptive and able to listen, in order to experience the concert fully. If the performer loses their focus, the audience is likely to as well.

Students are rather disconcerted when I can point to the bar where I know they lost focus. I can tell because it is exactly where I start drifting off as well.

Of course, I could drift off anyway, but if the performer is totally present and focused in every moment, as a listener, I am much more likely to stay engaged.

What unbalances this process of co-operation is when one is placed higher than another. We live in a culture that celebrates stardom, and none more so than in the world of music. People are impressed by the virtuoso who can play with extreme brilliance or the child prodigy who displays their talent earlier than others. The conductor who pulls the strands of the orchestral texture together, painting pictures in sound through the skill of the musicians in that orchestra, will be given more credit (and considerably more pay!) than the highly skilled, experienced members of the same orchestra. The performer, too, will often put the composer, especially the composers considered the 'greats', on a pedestal. By doing this, they are saying that the composer is bigger and better than they are. But each is part of a team and none, really, should be considered any better or more superior than another.

Music: the love song you play to yourself

Performance is often considered to be something you 'do' for other people and that you actively present. It doesn't need to be forced out or presented from a false sense of having to play for the audience, of needing to give to them in some way. The audience can pick up anything inauthentic even if they are not consciously aware of it, and they don't want to be performed *at*. An audience might be *interested* in how talented you are and how well you play your instrument. They might be impressed, or envious, or a whole range of emotions.

But deep down, whether they are aware of it or not, the audience is longing for the inspiration that can come through music, and the connection that it gives them to their own heart and soul.

Performing music is really a love song you play to yourself that you allow to be heard by other people. Imagine coming across someone playing the guitar to herself. She is captivated by the music, in love with the sounds she is hearing. She is in her own blissful world. That in turn becomes captivating. You find yourself drawn in, mesmerised by her playing. Before you know it, you are as absorbed as she is. You are not thinking about how talented she is or how well she plays her instrument. Instead, you are simply drawn into the music itself and you are being lifted by it. You are being nourished to the core of your being.

The power and beauty of vulnerability

Kathy showed me, possibly for the first time, the power and beauty of vulnerability. She was twenty and came with pains in her arms and wrists and all sorts of pianistic problems. She was a deeply sensitive person, and her emotional vulnerability showed. It showed in her face, which welled up with tears frequently, and more than that, it showed in her playing. Her playing was so moving that I was almost in tears myself. I felt moved in a way I hadn't been in years. She told me people regularly cried when she performed, as if it was the most natural thing in the world. And it was for her.

When someone plays from their heart and soul, when they are open, responsive, ready to express, and expectant to being moved and inspired, they can feel different.

They might suffer from nerves, but the nerves are not those that come from the Inner Critic or the pressure of only being as good as your last concert. These nerves come from a particular type of vulnerability. It is a vulnerability that comes from opening your heart and being yourself.

It comes from the ability to touch the audience, speak to them, share with them. It can be very wobbly. Your heart might pound, you might shake, you might feel breathless or you might have a lump in your throat. You are open to give. As the great jazz trumpeter Miles Davis said: "Sometimes you have to play a long time to be able to play like yourself."

'Touched by the Gods'

I remember going to a concert at the Wigmore Hall to hear a well-known string quartet. In the first half they played Haydn and early Beethoven, and in the second half they played Shostakovich. Maybe they weren't so keen on the Haydn and Beethoven, or maybe they were just passionate about Shostakovich. Whatever the reason, the second half came alive in a way that the first half hadn't. They lit up, came to life, played magnificently and with an energy and spirit that was captivating. It was one of those extraordinary performances that stand out. It was enough to bring a conservative British audience leaping to their feet at the end with whistles and shouts for more!

Any musician who has had this experience knows it and loves it. It is what draws them back again and again to the concert platform.

It is as if there is something bigger than the composer, music, musicians and audience. A magic "something" outside of us, that we want to capture, feel and treasure.

The musician who is out there performing has a knowledge of the music, their technique is in place and they are open and receptive. Then you feel as if you are not the performer actively playing the music, but that you are somehow *being played*. It is exhilarating, extraordinary and its effects are far-reaching. The player is lifted onto another level, and the audience, assuming they are equally open and receptive, are also lifted.

The Ancient Greeks and the Romans talked about this particular phenomenon as something 'outside' of themselves. It was something that came through you rather than being you, yourself. The Ancient Greeks called this the 'daimon' or 'muse' and the Romans called it 'genius'. It was something that might or might not visit. If it did, they recognised it as being 'touched by the gods' and celebrated it.

So what is this thing that is outside of ourselves which is not quite a part of us, and yet which comes through us? It is what a songwriter experiences when he is driving and some new lyrics hit him from out of nowhere, and he has to stop his car and write the words down on a scrap of paper; it is what Chopin experienced when he went into an excitable frenzy of composing, desperately trying to capture the elusive snatches of melody that he heard; it is what a chamber musician experiences when the whole group shares and plays at a whole new level of heightened awareness; or when a conductor is touched by the magic and the whole orchestra is taken out of themselves, inspired and elated, and the audience responds by going wild with applause.

This magic is something we can't quite identify. It doesn't behave rationally, it doesn't come when we expect it or demand it. When it does, it needs to be accepted and welcomed.

The magic only comes to fertile ground. It can come when you are prepared, ready, an open vessel with nothing blocking you.

It can come when your motivation is your own, when you release the blockage of negative beliefs and emotions, when you know how to manage your performance nerves. It can come when you have a physical freedom through body awareness, a deep and intimate knowledge of your instrument and the music you are playing. It can come when you are open and receptive to being inspired, ready and willing to create a moving and uplifting performance.

This is what it is to perform to the peak of your ability, to perform from your heart and soul. This is what it is to play music from the inside out.

Epilogue

Imagine yourself back as a young child again. There was something that inspired you towards music. Maybe your parents were musicians and you heard music all around you; maybe you were taken to a concert by an aunt or grandparent; you heard something on the radio and it lit you up inside. You wanted to dance around the room, express those delicious sounds in whatever way you knew how. The sounds were captivating, magical and you felt alive.

So either at your suggestion or your parents', music lessons came into the equation. It seemed a good thing to learn how to do what those adults could do to create music. You wanted to be like them, playing or singing. You wanted to join in and be part of it all. It was the easiest thing in the world. Music was your inspiration; it was calling you.

So you started having lessons, and if you were lucky, you had an inspirational teacher who brought it alive and made it fun. Whatever it was, you kept going and you became better and better, more and more skilled at the instrument you had chosen. Other children seemed to fall by the wayside, not interested in lessons, possibly not inspired by their teacher. But it was different for you. You were now very good and were getting a lot of attention for being very good.

You carried on making progress, your teacher was pleased and your parents were proud. The hours you had to practise got longer, you felt you had to choose practising over seeing your friends in order to prepare for a competition, exam or festival that your teacher said was important. The pressure from outside was hotting up. Competition followed competition and you starting feeling as if you were on a conveyor belt, but you didn't feel you could do anything about it. And you were getting so much attention. You were told you were exceptionally talented, so a new teacher was found for you – the best in the country. This teacher was ruthless, demanding even longer hours of practice. She demanded perfection, and anything less was not good enough. She would shout at you and tell you that you were not applying yourself, not trying hard enough and that you would never 'make it' if you didn't make sacrifices and work harder. You started doubting yourself, feeling as if you must secretly be terrible, in essence a fraud. Everything was becoming a chore. Bit by bit, the flame of inspiration was dying out.

You were now at a music, college doing well, winning prizes, opportunities coming your way, and yet underneath, the lack of self-belief was intensifying. Performing was becoming a struggle. Your nerves were a problem. In your last concert, you had had a major memory slip and you felt you had failed your teacher. You imagined your contemporaries talking about you.

And then the last straw: you noticed a pain in your wrist when you played. You worried incessantly about it, desperately wanting reassurance, but equally not wanting to talk about it. To own up to it felt like death to your playing and your future career as a musician. The doctor said it was tendonitis, that you needed rest for six weeks and that if nothing improved, to consider an operation. Not only would you have to give up your hard-won concerto with the college symphony orchestra, but you had to stop playing for six weeks. Six weeks! You hadn't done that since you were four years old. How would you cope? Would an operation wreck your hands? What was your life all about now? Would you ever play again? How had it all come to this?

So now you realise that you have hit a turning point. You either have to get yourself back on track or you risk having to choose a different career. What do you choose?

You decide that you are going to give this everything you have. You are going to invest in yourself. Other people have always invested in your talent and ability in the past, but now you are going to invest in yourself. You are going to get help in whatever shape that might come. You glean information from everywhere you can, scouring the Internet for ideas, talking to close friends. You start reading anything that resonates with how you are thinking, you are open and receptive to whatever might come your way.

And it does! Someone you don't know that well shows you how negative your thought patterns are. You find this extremely uncomfortable at first. Why are they saying these things? You hardly know this person, and yet somewhere inside you, you know this is important and that you need to listen. The more you listen, the more amazed you are. You had no idea you were thinking like this. This person you didn't know very well turns into a friend and you discover you have incredible support from the friendship.

You find yourself drawn towards an improvisation group. This is something you have never done before and you feel nervous. Your wrists are still causing you pain, so you precede with caution. After about an hour, you start to relax and realise it can be quite fun. You don't have to be 'perfect'; no-one has any expectations of you. It feels to you as if you are just 'messing around', and that feels wonderfully freeing. You stay for two hours 'messing around' and then realise that you have had next to no pain for that entire time! It dawns on you that you are letting go of a pressure that has been with you everyday since you were a young child. Does that have something to do with the build-up to the pain in the first place, you wonder?

You decide to look into The Alexander Technique. It has never really appealed to you before, but this time you have an inspirational teacher. Who shows you how to balance and free your entire way of holding yourself. You realise you are locking your wrists and elbows, and you start, bit by bit, to let go of that tension.

You decide through your own volition that you will take two months off anything that you feel is pressurising. You pull out of a big competition, reassuring yourself that you will be able to do it next year instead. Your teacher is not entirely happy because they know you are almost certain to win it. But you feel galvanised and empowered by your new discoveries, and you decide that you will do what is best for you, whatever anyone else says.

You ease up your playing completely. You start revisiting basic technique and realise that you had never thought about it before. Your teacher starts coming round to the idea that you need time, and becomes supportive to your journey. They work with you patiently, allowing you to find your own way and discover new ways of playing that are much freer and more efficient.

It is now the summer and you make a radical decision. You will take time off and you will travel, not for concerts or competitions, but for fun. You go with your new friend and you go away for an entire month. No practising for a month. You have never, ever had a break for so long. You look back to when the GP told you that you needed to stop playing for six weeks, and how you had panicked. Now you are relishing the idea.

You are back from your trip and you decide to pick up your instrument. You feel a little flutter of nervousness but it feels good to connect. You start to play and you realise that the pain has gone. You tentatively start playing a difficult study with all the new freedoms that you have learnt, and you realise that this is now going to be possible. This has whetted your appetite and now you really want to play. You take all the music you can find, and play and play. You absolutely love it. You want to play all day and all night, and you probably would except that a cautious part of you doesn't want to risk getting pain again.

You are back! You are back again to your instrument and to the world of music. The pain that had been so devastating just a few months ago has almost entirely gone. Gradually, you build up your playing again. You discover that you are enjoying playing more than you can ever remember. A concert comes your way and you feel ready for it now. You go on stage, you feel good, calm, self-assured. You play and something extraordinary happens. You feel as if you are not playing at all. Something is flowing through you. It is you, and yet it is not you. You don't understand it and you just go with it. It feels so amazing. You are performing, expressing yourself — and it has never felt so good!

Printed in Great Britain
by Amazon